I0048553

Praise for *S.O.A.P. for Success*

"This guide to the S.O.A.P. methodology is a must-read for mission-driven entrepreneurs and small-business owners seeking a clear, structured path to operational excellence. By adapting a time-tested clinical framework to the business world, Dr. West provides a practical and intuitive tool for diagnosing challenges, prioritizing problems, and developing actionable solutions—all while staying true to the heart of a business's mission. Whether you're running a veterinary clinic or launching a new venture, this approach will sharpen your focus, elevate your leadership, and reignite your passion for the work you do."

—**KATHERINE FITZGERALD**, DVM, Dean of
Veterinary Sciences, Trocaire College

"As both an economist and a business leader, I'm drawn to tools that cut through complexity and drive meaningful action. In *S.O.A.P. for Success*, Dr. Stephanie West brilliantly applies a diagnostic method familiar to healthcare—and refreshingly powerful in business. Like a skilled clinician, she teaches leaders to gather the right data, make clear assessments, and implement plans that deliver real results. This book is a must-read for any entrepreneur or executive ready to diagnose their business challenges and revitalize their mission with precision, clarity, and purpose."

—**MATTHEW SALOIS**, PhD, President, Veterinary
Management Groups; former
Chief Economist, American
Veterinary Medical Association

"Dr. West has had a remarkable career leading mission-driven veterinary organizations to fulfill their mission and enjoy financial success. In various leadership roles, she's proven that mission and margin can coexist, and that purpose and passion do not have to come at the expense of profit. Her proven techniques have applications well beyond the veterinary world. Dr. West has consistently turned around struggling businesses by utilizing a time-honored medical problem-solving methodology called S.O.A.P. This simple-to-use formula quickly evaluates, gets to the heart of the issue, and develops solutions. This book is for you if you are looking to simplify your organization's management, stay true to your mission, and grow your business."

—DR. BOB LESTER, DVM, Cofounder and Chief Medical Officer, WellHaven Pet Health

"Many of us leading mission-driven businesses are fueled by passion, not a formal business degree, a challenge I've discussed with Dr. Stephanie West over the years. Her solution, *S.O.A.P. for Success*, is a brilliant and approachable guide that translates the logic of the time-tested clinical S.O.A.P. framework into a powerful system for business health. The result is a must-read for veterinarians, or really any business leader, seeking to grow their impact!"

—DR. CALEB FRANKEL, VMD, ER Veterinarian, Founder and CEO of Instinct Science

"Dr. West delivers a straightforward yet powerful approach that speaks the language of veterinary professionals. Rooted in the diagnostic mindset we use every day in veterinary medicine, this strategy helps veterinarians assess their businesses—and their lives—with the same clarity and confidence they bring to patient care."

—DAN GROOMS, DVM, PhD, Stephen G. Juelsgaard Dean, Iowa State University College of Veterinary Medicine

"I had the opportunity to work with Stephanie during the acquisition and transition of her clinic, and I saw firsthand her rare ability to lead with both heart and operational clarity. In this book, she brings that same balance to the page—making business principles accessible through real stories and a practical framework drawn from the clinical world: S.O.A.P.—Subjective, Objective, Assessment, and Plan. It's the perfect model for thoughtful, mission-driven leaders who want to improve their operations without losing sight of their purpose. This book is a refreshing, honest, and genuinely helpful guide for anyone navigating the business side of caring professions."

—DR. NICHOLAS NELSON, DVM, MBA,
president, BluePearl Specialty and
Emergency Pet Hospital

S.O.A.P.

FOR

SUCCESS

A SIMPLE METHOD TO MANAGE YOUR
BUSINESS AND REVITALIZE YOUR MISSION

DR. STEPHANIE F. WEST

RIVER GROVE
BOOKS

This publication is designed to provide accurate and authoritative information in regard to the subject matter covered. It is sold with the understanding that the publisher and author are not engaged in rendering legal, accounting, or other professional services. Nothing herein shall create an attorney-client relationship, and nothing herein shall constitute legal advice or a solicitation to offer legal advice. If legal advice or other expert assistance is required, the services of a competent professional should be sought.

Published by River Grove Books
Austin, TX
www.rivergrovebooks.com

Copyright © 2025 Stephanie West

All rights reserved.

Thank you for purchasing an authorized edition of this book and for complying with copyright law. No part of this book may be reproduced, stored in a retrieval system, or transmitted by any means, electronic, mechanical, photocopying, recording, or otherwise, without written permission from the copyright holder.

Distributed by River Grove Books

Design and composition by Greenleaf Book Group and Sheila Parr
Cover design by Greenleaf Book Group and Sheila Parr

Publisher's Cataloging-in-Publication data is available.

Print ISBN: 978-1-966629-29-0

eBook ISBN: 978-1-966629-30-6

First Edition

To Greg, my beloved husband,
for food, laughter, and love.

CONTENTS

INTRODUCTION

———

WHEN YOUR MISSION IS ALSO A BUSINESS

Most businesses serve others in some way. Whether they make or sell goods or services, they likely wouldn't exist if they weren't meeting a need that someone, somewhere was willing to pay for. In this way, all entrepreneurs, small-business owners, and workplace leaders are driven by a purpose—an intrinsic mission.

What this mission is will invariably differ from business to business. While all companies aim to generate profit, some claim this as their only goal. For these companies, the unwavering focus will be on managerial staff with formal training, streamlined business practices, and strict bottom lines. Yet, for other companies, the mission may be more metaphysical in nature: a desire to provide healthcare to pets or care and housing for the elderly, a passion for creating food, or a knack for interior decoration, among many others.

If your business falls into the latter category, and passion motivates you more than profit, you're going to want to keep reading. You may have created your small business from scratch, or you may have started at the ground floor and worked your way up to management. These unconventional paths to business leadership may mean you may have little formal training in management, leaving you to learn while doing. As you keep your business's underlying mission alive each day, you're also striving to understand how to run a business.

I am lucky enough to have met many entrepreneurs and small-business owners over the years. I find them passionate and proud of their businesses, but sometimes they feel trapped by the day-to-day operational tasks required to run a business, such as filing quarterly taxes, meeting payroll, managing online reviews, and overseeing the facilities and utilities.

If this feels familiar, you may welcome a way to get control of all the management details quickly so you can return to fulfilling your purpose for going into business in the first place. You may strongly believe in your mission and feel torn between fulfilling it and meeting the administrative needs of the business. Running a business can seem overwhelming, and analyzing how that business is doing can be a daunting but critical task.

This book offers a simple-to-use formula for evaluating your business and getting to the heart of issues quickly, allowing you to create a rapid and effective action plan—no special management training needed.

I know this formula works because I've used it myself. I started out as a veterinarian in a field where it is common to start a practice with little to no formal business training. Veterinary practices are typically started by veterinarians who deeply love their mission to serve their animal patients, but they soon find that a business does not run on love and mission alone.

These veterinarians often end up neck-deep in responsibilities—employees, a facility, inventory, equipment—and suddenly, the needs of running the business are pulling them away from their beloved practice of veterinary medicine. They typically need to hire help, maybe in the form of another veterinarian who can see patients while the owner handles management, or maybe a practice manager, which will allow the owner to return to practicing the medicine they love. But even with such help, the owner still needs a way to oversee the health of their practice.

My story in veterinary management started much this way. After a year of practicing as an associate veterinarian, split between a couple of sole-owner veterinarians, I accepted a position at an urban practice as the associate veterinarian. The owner explained that she had recently opened a second location in the suburbs, where a second associate veterinarian worked. She was trying to make both locations financially viable while still wanting to practice as a veterinarian herself. She had two businesses where she and two associate veterinarians saw patients, and she then somehow had to manage both clinics. Her business techniques and decisions were good, but she couldn't be in two places at once. She ran the larger clinic and found the satellite clinic was suffering as a result. She asked me to manage the second clinic while she oversaw the main office.

With my scientific and logical training as a veterinarian, I automatically began analyzing the business like a medical professional would evaluate a patient. I looked for obvious issues, with the first being that the clinic was not making enough revenue to pay for itself. If I couldn't turn this into a profitable clinic, the satellite would need to close. I had identified the main problem, which would then guide my further research and actions. This is a critical first step in analyzing your business, similar to a doctor reviewing a patient record—what is wrong, or what do you want to improve or change?

Over time, I have realized that the thought process I use to diagnose and treat patients can also be effectively applied to a business. Just as a patient has multiple body systems—cardiovascular, gastrointestinal, respiratory, etc.—a business has multiple departments or units—human resources, inventory, financial, operations, etc.—and the same easy-to-learn logic that doctors rely on can also support business leaders in running their companies.

In the decades since I first started my management journey, I have used this tool effectively as a veterinary administrator to assess multiple veterinary-related businesses, including a small general practice, a large emergency clinic, an academic veterinary technology program, and in multiple teaching hospitals at a college of veterinary medicine.

I call this tool S.O.A.P., an acronym used in the medical community, which stands for Subjective data, Objective data, Assessment, and Plan. With this tool, you can easily identify and then treat what might be ailing your business. In the upcoming pages, I walk you through these steps and share real-life examples of businesses I have improved using this quick and useful thought process.

The S.O.A.P. tool can be easily scaled up or down to fit the size and needs of your business, including a changing business climate. And it can help you handle unexpected challenges (such as a global pandemic!) in a logical and effective manner.

This book is for anyone who loves the business they lead but wants a simple process so they can manage it more easily. My method will help these leaders cut through confusing details and organize an action plan that will free them up to focus once again on fulfilling the mission they believe in.

PART I

S.O.A.P. AS A METHODOLOGY FOR BUSINESS

1

WHAT IS S.O.A.P.?

Learning how to view a business and its ailments the same way a veterinarian would view sick patients—analyze, diagnose, and treat—allows you to apply this same methodology to your business, regardless of your business management experience (or lack thereof), to quickly identify issues and develop a logical action plan. In my career as a veterinarian treating animals and managing veterinary-related businesses, I've used this technique across different business models (small businesses, academic institutions, and corporations), and it has never failed to help me assess and follow through in helping a business meet its mission and goals. Here's how the process works.

S.O.A.P.: SUBJECTIVE, OBJECTIVE, ASSESSMENT, PLAN

When I start working with a business, I first apply a basic tool from medicine that I learned in school: the Problem-Oriented Veterinary Medical Record using the S.O.A.P. (subjective, objective, assessment, plan) process. This is a method of analysis to find abnormalities or issues, list them in a problem list, and then track and treat those problems. In essence, I treat the business the way I approach an animal patient, with a logical thought process to review and speedily identify key action steps that will make the most difference.

In veterinary medicine, we evaluate our animal patients using a formal examination pattern based on their body system—heart and circulatory system, stomach and intestinal system, skin, eyes and ears, and so on. We include subjective findings (does the animal seem to be in pain and depressed or happy and relaxed?) and objective findings (heart and respiratory rate, results of an eye exam, color of the mucous membranes) in our evaluation. Any abnormalities identified are written on a problem list. All issues found, whether large or small, are placed on this list, which is then reviewed and analyzed. The analysis leads to potential diagnostic steps to find more information or treatment steps—the plan—to resolve the issue. Following the plan will yield more information and, hopefully, an improvement for the patient. The logic of being "problem-oriented" means that no issues are missed, and it tends to result in better patient outcomes.

You can treat a business the same way: as one entity with

multiple systems, such as revenue, expenses, facility, clients, etc. This enables you to leverage the same technique used by medical professionals (both human and veterinary) to effectively and efficiently "diagnose" and "treat" the business. This problem-oriented technique quickly identifies key issues for the business to correct, and the method I use to evaluate the business is the same S.O.A.P. process I use for my veterinary patients.

This problem-oriented approach first appeared in the 1960s, when the human medical profession started using the "Problem-Oriented Medical Record" devised by Yale professor Dr. Lawrence Weed, who sought to improve medical record-keeping by identifying and documenting specific issues in a logical manner.[1] Before this, patient records were often haphazard and inconsistent. Dr. Weed's system required the doctor to work methodically. First, the doctor would ask questions of their patients to determine a history of the issue and specifics of how they felt (*subjective* data). Then, the doctor would carefully examine their patient in a systematic manner, including diagnostic tests or procedures (*objective* data). After that, the doctor would fully document the examination, identifying and listing specific problems that needed to be addressed (*assessment*). Finally, the doctor would decide the next steps in diagnosing or treating the patient (*plan*).

---

1. Weed, L. L. "Medical Records, Patient Care, and Medical Education." *Irish Journal of Medical Science* 39 (1964): 271–282. https://doi.org/10.1007/BF02945791.

Once the plan was implemented, there would be new data: The patient could have been feeling better, a test result might have changed to negative or positive, and a new analysis or assessment of the patient would occur. This second analysis was called a "progress report" and was an important step in the process. Each progress report would result in an updated plan, triggering additional data, new analysis, and so on. This pattern would continue until the issue was—hopefully—resolved or an ongoing treatment plan was created to help the patient if the issue couldn't be cured completely.

Dr. Weed named these ongoing progress reports S.O.A.P. notes. Using this system, the physician progresses sequentially through each step, documenting their thought process until a medical record has been generated that can be easily understood by any subsequent doctor evaluating the case or treating the patient.

This plan included an essential tool called the "problem list," which captured all issues in one place. These problems could be large or small, related or unrelated, but by listing all of them in one place, there was less chance of overlooking any issues. Problems that were resolved would be marked with the date and moved to a "resolved" section and removed from the active problem list, but they were always available for the next doctor to review in case the issue recurred. Overall, this type of logical documentation greatly improved medicine by decreasing the human memory factor of the individual doctor and allowing for systematic analysis of documented treatments that could be shared with other doctors.

The veterinary field realized the benefits of this methodical system, but it needed slight modifications since, unlike human patients, veterinary patients can't tell the veterinarian where it hurts or what is wrong. While the subjective aspect in human medicine primarily includes the symptoms described by the patient about how they feel, it's harder with animals. Veterinarians need to analyze and interpret the patient's body language and physical signs and take information from the animal's owner— who may or may not be a good observer or understand medical issues. Because this subjective information doesn't come directly from the patient, the veterinary world replaces the word "symptoms" with "signs," which highlights that it may not be accurate, but it's what appears to be happening.

Taking the S.O.A.P. method beyond the veterinary exam room and into my management "toolbox," I've found that using the same process to analyze a business works just as well as using it to examine and treat an animal patient.

I start with the "S" and inquire about subjective data. Of course, the business can't directly tell me what is wrong, but there are suspicious signs that an alert owner or a manager can notice. These subjective aspects include things like the overall culture, reputation, and how customers and employees feel about the business.

Moving on to the "O" in S.O.A.P., I review the objective

data. There are a lot of objective data points in business: financial reports, key performance indicators (KPIs), and the like.

Using the data obtained from the subjective and objective data collection, I then work with the "A"—assessment—and identify specific problems to be solved.

Now it's time for the "P"—the action plan—created for each individual business or business unit to guide the owner or manager to the next steps that will bring the business back to optimum functioning. This yields pertinent and actionable information to deal with the problems identified and track progress. So it is a "problem-oriented" method of running your business for optimal "health"!

TAKEAWAYS

- S.O.A.P. stands for Subjective, Objective, Assessment, and Plan.

- The S.O.A.P. method describes a process by which medical doctors create a written record for a patient, capturing how the patient feels (subjective), their symptoms (objective), the doctor's assessment, and the treatment plan.

- The issues identified are captured in a problem list and analyzed for patterns and action steps. This makes it a problem-oriented record, supporting a logical process with pertinent action steps that tie directly back to problems identified for effective management of the patient (or business!).

2

USING S.O.A.P. FOR
YOUR BUSINESS

The problem-oriented S.O.A.P. process supports logic and analysis, which can be extremely helpful in managing a business. Let me show you how I used this approach—creating a S.O.A.P. problem list—with a business in dire need of a turnaround. (The results of this S.O.A.P. business tale are discussed further in Chapter 4.)

Several years ago, I was approached by a veterinary emergency clinic that was not performing as expected. The shareholders knew there was a healthy demand for the services, yet the financial return on investment was minimal to nonexistent. Shareholders had not seen any profit despite paying for a modern facility and great doctors. I was tasked with evaluating and correcting the issues holding it back.

This hospital had been created decades earlier as a shareholder corporation by most of the local veterinary practice owners, who built a separate hospital and hired emergency veterinarians to handle the overnight emergencies for all the clinics in the area rather than having each veterinary hospital do this individually, which required a staff veterinarian to come in at night or on weekends after working all day.

The concept was widely known to be effective, but this clinic had been just squeaking by for years. They hadn't turned a profit despite the shareholders investing in good staff and the latest equipment. The shareholders hired me to see what issues I could identify and fix. Naturally, I utilized the problem-oriented approach and the S.O.A.P. format to evaluate the business.

STARTING WITH THE "S"—SUBJECTIVE

First, I looked at the subjective aspects. In general, what I include here is anything that isn't exactly quantifiable but is important to one or more of the stakeholders. For this veterinary emergency clinic, I identified the stakeholders as the shareholders, the employee veterinarians, the staff, the pet patients, and the pet owners. To get this information, you can use client satisfaction or employee engagement surveys, read online reviews, conduct in-person staff "stay" interviews, perform an assessment of the culture, and the like.

I learned that the clinic had a mixed reputation among the shareholder veterinarians who referred their clients to that clinic and didn't always receive timely reports, although it had a better reputation with clients who were generally happy with the emergency veterinary care. The staff I interviewed had a lot of varied, small individual complaints, but I also heard consistent rumblings of discontent with the hospital director, a long-time manager who always seemed to say the right thing but whose actions didn't seem to match his promises or assurances to the staff.

IDENTIFYING THE "O"—OBJECTIVE

Next, I dove into the objective aspects, which included facts and data. For this aspect, I looked into the physical building and parking lot, examined the inventory and equipment, and reviewed the financial statements. I hit an immediate snag because, at the time, there were no industry financial benchmarks for emergency veterinary practices, just for general practice of routine care for dogs and cats.

Every business has benchmarks, which are the expected percentages of revenue for each type of expense. General veterinary practices have to carry a lot of routine care inventory and supplies, like vaccinations and medications, that aren't part of emergency care at all. Accordingly, I saw that the expense category was very low for such inventory. That made sense, but other expense categories were much higher than I had seen in routine practice. Was this normal or an aberration? At the time, I didn't know, so that was definitely another problem to add to my list for future follow-up.

MAKING THE "A"—ASSESSMENT

This led me to the assessment phase. Here, I listed all of the issues I had discovered, whether big or small, and then ranked them in importance and difficulty. This ranking was an important part of the assessment. Some issues, like not having industry standards for the financial benchmarks, were both important and difficult, so I would need to address them later in a formal plan. Other concerns were minor or easy to fix, and they simply needed to be handled as quickly as possible.

For instance, there were a couple of staff complaints that were fairly minor in the big scheme—clipper blades that weren't sharp enough and missing coffee in the staff break room—but were easily addressed and made a huge improvement in the subjective aspect of staff morale. This points out the importance of listing all the problems identified, whether large or small. Without the S.O.A.P. format, I would likely have started digging into the big issue of the financial benchmarks, which I did, but I would probably have ignored the smaller issues and would have missed the chance to improve staff morale.

I then reviewed all the problems we identified, ranked them according to importance, and determined whether I saw patterns that might indicate other underlying issues.

LANDING ON THE "P"—PLAN

My initial plan included quickly fixing as many of the small, individual complaints as I could within the limited budget to improve staff morale. This gave me instant credibility with the staff, as they saw me as a manager who would take prompt action. Other issues weren't as easy to fix. I was unfamiliar with the software used by the veterinary practice, so I had an action step to personally learn how to use key features of the system.

Additionally, a big problem was the lack of industry benchmarks for veterinary emergency clinic financials or KPIs. Most veterinary financial benchmarks were for general veterinary practices for pets, not emergency clinics. It became quickly obvious to me that the emergency clinic, as a surprisingly different business model, did not fit the published industry recommendations. For example, a typical well-managed veterinary general practice might have 20 percent of its expenses tied up in inventory, as they have drugs available for treating multiple conditions and long-term illnesses, but emergency medicine needed very few medications, so inventory was a much smaller percent. However, good emergency medical care required significant staffing, so the financial percentage of payroll was much higher than the normal accepted industry standard.

When I reviewed the financial statements, they were very different from what I had expected based on a general practice, but without benchmarks, I didn't know what may be an issue and what was "normal" for an emergency practice. While this lack wasn't something I could quickly change, I joined a society for veterinary business managers and began to network with others to lobby for the industry to start collecting this data.

Being unable to compare industry benchmarks led me to an action plan of reviewing the financial statements over time, so I could compare the months and years over time to see if there were any discrepancies. This turned out to be the key that unlocked a significant issue, as discussed in Chapter 4.

WHAT TO CONSIDER WHEN APPLYING S.O.A.P. TO A BUSINESS

Now that we've seen how the application of S.O.A.P. worked in one specific instance, let's step back and look at the four components in broader terms. Here are more ideas for how you can identify each one.

Subjective

All businesses have a subjective component because people are involved, and people have feelings, perceptions, likes, and dislikes. To evaluate what subjective measurements can be followed in your business, it is helpful to identify stakeholders. These are people who interact with your business in some manner. Some are obvious, and others less so.

- **Ownership Personnel:** This group can be as small as an individual or grow to include a board, shareholders, or investors.

- **Employees:** These range from a solo owner-operator to the huge staff of a global institution or corporation.

- **Suppliers and Vendors:** These may also be included in some instances.

- **Customers, Clients, and Students:** This includes all other terms for the people served by the business.

- **Culture of the Business:** This is the "feel" of the business as noted by employees who work there, customers and clients, its reputation in the community, and any media presence, whether overt (such as an advertising campaign) or covert (such as word of mouth).

Analyzing the subjective aspects of a business can include conversations with the stakeholders, employee engagement surveys, exit interviews with employees who have given notice, client satisfaction surveys, net promoter scores, and online review ratings. But the very concept that it is subjective means that these things can be difficult to quantify. Because of that, the subjective aspects have traditionally been difficult to measure, study, or change. Historically, this was part of the goodwill or reputation of a business that may have been a factor argued over during a sale but rarely quantified into any action step.

However, in an age of online marketing, social media, and digital information, there are far more tools for manipulating subjective factors available to those who run a business than before the digital age. There are also more risks as a local business issue can be amplified to a national or even global level by a single negative post that goes "viral." A business that tries to ignore subjective factors these days will likely underperform a business that includes them in planning and operations.

Objective

Collecting objective data is typically a large focus of management training. You may have heard that "what can be measured can be managed" or other such maxims. It is generally true that if something isn't looked for, it is less likely to be seen—and probably will not be addressed.

In veterinary medicine, this is the reason veterinarians are trained to perform a full physical exam on most patients, even if the patient presents with a specific problem that appears localized to one area. A full physical exam includes a review of all the body systems that the veterinarian can touch, see, listen to, or otherwise investigate in a noninvasive manner. Any veterinarian could share stories of unexpected medical issues found due to a thorough medical exam.

Early in my career, I remember meeting a new client with two cats who came in for routine physical exams and vaccinations. In my physical exam of the first cat, I discovered that her lungs weren't moving air well, and we quickly followed up to find and address a serious problem where the lungs were filling with fluid. Turning to the other cat, I was shocked to find a serious issue on his exam as well. While it is unusual to find two different unexpected major issues in two patients from the same household, I never forgot the importance of a full physical exam, even if the patients appeared normal from the outside.

Like my veterinary patients, your business also needs a regular examination. Just like the body systems of the veterinary patient, your business has many different aspects that can and should be measured and monitored. While it may be tempting to simply go with the flow if the business appears to be making money and running well, there are many horror stories of businesses suddenly failing because of unseen issues. It is important to perform a regular review of your business, tracking various aspects so you can monitor trends and anticipate potential issues early enough to prevent or mitigate them.

Depending on the size of the business, this exam may take place daily, weekly, monthly, quarterly, or on whatever schedule works best for you. It is important to take the time and set up a structure to capture the objective data important to your business. Examples of what to include in this exam could be a walk-through inspection of the physical plant or facility and associated grounds, storage units, or vehicles. Internally, this could include checking on current inventory, supplies, and equipment types and amounts.

Financial data is a fairly easy method to review many important business systems, but it requires an appropriate chart of accounts and financial bookkeeping to make the financial data relevant and accurate. Records and record-keeping systems would also be an aspect to review. Staffing numbers, benefits, and associated costs are important, but so are staff turnover rates and other measures. Even supply chain issues and the overall economy may be part of the objective data reviewed by a savvy business manager or owner. This information should be captured in a format that can be tracked over time to identify trends. (Yes, spreadsheets can be your friends!)

Assessment

My next step is to make the "assessment"—to review all the problems identified, according to the ranking, and see if any patterns might indicate the underlying issue. This is a key aspect of the problem-oriented approach to managing your business. Without this step, you have simply gathered a huge list of issues that could become an overwhelming and depressing to-do list. This assessment phase is the step that is most often ignored, to the detriment of the business. However, if effectively utilized, the assessment phase is the key to unlocking the most important actions that will make the most profound differences for your business.

Assessment requires you to sit back a bit and review your problem list as a whole, looking for these patterns or similarities. You may want to group certain problems together, for instance, by department, manager, timeframe, or other similarity. I like spreadsheets that can be sorted by different factors so that I can start to see patterns.

For instance, in a business with the two different problems of poor staff morale and a high overtime pay expense, it is possible that forced overtime is making staff unhappy, or alternatively, the connection could be that unhappy staff were calling out sick a lot, which required dedicated staff to work overtime to compensate. By looking for a connection, you may find the deep underlying cause to work on (forced overtime or excessive sick callouts in this example). If you can work on the deeper cause, the other problems may fix themselves.

For instance, if you had identified high overtime was caused by excessive sick callouts, forcing others to work overtime, addressing the staff morale problem and halting the callouts would decrease or possibly eliminate the issue of the compensatory overtime. Not all of those patterns are evident, but by reviewing all the problems, potential issues come to light that may otherwise have been hidden.

These possible patterns or potential causes are similar to the differential diagnoses in medicine—possible but not definitive causes of the issues. In a veterinary medical example, if the patient had been noted as drinking a lot of water, and also urinating a lot, it is known that these two signs often appear together and can indicate illnesses such as kidney disease or diabetes mellitus, so they would then be on the differential diagnosis list as possible diseases to test for. This review then informs and leads directly to the action part of the plan. Your assessment will also lead you directly to the important plan that is tailored to your business.

Plan

For each problem or group of problems, you will want to develop an action plan—the actions you want the business to take to overcome the primary problems you've identified. In an initial assessment with a lot of issues, the plan may even include a "not now" section. Even if an issue isn't a high priority now, you don't want to forget it. Usually, issues on the "not now" list will resurface in importance until they are also handled.

For example, in a veterinary patient, if the veterinarian sees a dog with a broken leg, who is bleeding a lot from several wounds and is very weak but also has fleas and a skin allergy, all of those problems would be noted, but the veterinarian would deal with the most critical issue first, which is the active bleeding. Once the bleeding is stopped, the weakness should improve over time as the patient gets supportive care and becomes metabolically stable. At that point, the dog should be strong enough to have surgery for the broken leg.

If surgery was performed while the dog was still actively bleeding and weak, he may not have been strong enough to survive the surgery, so this ranking of problems is very critical. To continue with this example, the problem of fleas and skin allergy shouldn't be forgotten but may not be fully addressed until the other issues are dealt with. The S.O.A.P. format allows the veterinarian to keep track of all the ranked issues and get them handled in the appropriate order while leaving no problem forgotten. For your business, any pain points will be captured and evaluated so they don't get lost.

The plan is not a set document; it will change over time. The initial plan includes actions, and once those actions are taken, the S.O.A.P. process is performed again. This is why another name for the S.O.A.P. is "progress notes." You progress along the plan and revise each time.

In the prior veterinary example, after the bleeding was stopped, the patient would be assessed again with a revised S.O.A.P. The problem of active bleeding would be marked resolved, which allows the next-ranked problem of weakness to rise up in importance. Likewise, when using S.O.A.P. for a business, identifying and then ranking the problems will help an owner or manager address issues that will make the most difference or provide the quickest results.

TURNING TO TRIAGE

The S.O.A.P. format can be scaled up or down as needed, providing a big-picture view or delving into a specific department or unit. The advantage of this plan is a logical evaluation of the area to be examined, with a documented problem list and action plan for effective action, delegation, and follow-up. It is a tool that provides a clear framework that decreases the chances of missing a key issue and helps drive effective results.

An essential aspect of the S.O.A.P. method is the concept of triage. In medicine, triage is a ranking of problems based on medical severity. As implied in the example of the dog with the bleeding, the broken leg, and the fleas, the problems in the individual patient can be triaged and addressed in order of medical importance. In a larger hospital setting with multiple patients, the medical staff may also need to triage individual patients. In an emergency setting, patients would be seen in order of medical issue risk. For instance, if the three problems of bleeding, broken limb, and fleas were individual problems of three different patients, the bleeding patient would be seen first, even if the patient with fleas arrived earlier, based on the triage or prioritization.

Your business problems can likewise be triaged. There are multiple methods of prioritizing a large problem list. Obviously, problems that are likely to cause business failure if not immediately addressed would go first. For instance, if the business suddenly were the subject of cyberbullying on social media, which can seriously and quickly create an adverse and unsafe work environment and dramatically drop client confidence in the business, that would warrant an immediate and robust response. The business would likely need to pull resources from other areas to deal with this serious threat to the subjective aspect (reputation and working environment) until the situation was appropriately handled.

PROBLEM LIST

Luckily, most problems are not of the magnitude to threaten immediate failure, but many can cause a slow drain of vital resources, reputation, culture, or operational integrity and still must be addressed. This points to the importance of capturing all problems, big or small, in a problem list.

This list is separate from, but a critical ancillary aspect of, the S.O.A.P. methodology. At each phase of the S.O.A.P., problems will be identified, modified, or resolved. The problem list will initially be a quick list of everything you've noted about the business, whether the problem is big or small. Depending on the size of your business, you can either make a simple list or categorize items into specific areas. When I managed a large institution with multiple hospitals, I had problem lists divided into multiple areas, based on the appropriate team that would need to handle it (personnel, legal, medical, facilities, operations, media, etc.), but when running a small practice, I only needed one simple list.

During the analysis phase, it is important to review the entire problem list to look for patterns and potential links. For instance, in one location I reviewed, a problem with an increased number of workers' compensation cases was due to increased bite wound injuries. Further review identified a staff shortage that led to experienced yet overworked staff not always paying attention to safety protocols, plus an increase in new, less-trained employees. Implementing bite safety training helped improve the training of new hires, which led to less overwork by experienced staff and decreased the workers' compensation claims. Additionally, the subjective morale of the staff in the area improved. Because of this analysis, multiple problems on the list were addressed with one solution.

TAKEAWAYS

- Your business management can utilize the problem-oriented S.O.A.P. method to support a logical process for strategic and operational excellence.

- **Subjective** aspects of your business would include how people feel about your business. This can be clients and customers, employees, or your public and online reputation. Any issues you find will be added to your problem list.

- **Objective** aspects of your business would be things you can see or measure, such as the facilities, inventory, finances, and equipment. Findings or issues identified would be added to your problem list.

- **Assessment** is the critical step of reviewing the findings from the problem list you created from your subjective and objective data collection. Here is where you will identify action steps for your operational and strategic plan.

- **Plan** is the summation of the action steps that will either clarify or correct the problems you have identified. These can be ordered (triaged) by importance.

- The **problem list** is where you record the findings from your subjective and objective review, which is then used for your assessment and plan follow-up.

- Using the problem-oriented S.O.A.P. method allows you to **treat a business like a patient**, diagnosing issues and prescribing appropriate steps to address them.

PART II

S.O.A.P. IN ACTION

3

IT STARTED WITH A CANDY BAR

I t's odd how a sweet tooth helped to turn around an entire business. I was only a few years out of veterinary school, working as an associate veterinarian in the main clinic of a two-location veterinary practice in a midsize city. I had an entrepreneurial spirit, so when my boss offered me the chance to try and save the other location—a failing satellite clinic in the suburbs—I jumped at it. My additional compensation would be based on my success: either 2 percent of any increase I mustered in gross revenue or nothing if I failed to turn things around.

The bar was pretty low: This satellite clinic had never done well from the day it opened. My boss was already resigned to having to close it, so failure on my part had no real consequences. But as a single mom carrying the kind of hefty student loan debt common in the veterinary world, the thought of that potential

2 percent of any increase in overall gross income to boost my salary was intriguing.

A FAILING SATELLITE CLINIC

The satellite clinic had moved from a strip mall to a free-standing building, hoping to gain more visibility, but business still wasn't taking off. The main clinic in the city had a good reputation, so we might assume people in the suburbs would have been willing to seek out the more proximate location. But there just weren't a lot of clients coming in.

When I started working at the satellite clinic, I noticed that a few animal patients were dropped off in the mornings for procedures, and then nothing was scheduled for the rest of the day until 5:00 p.m., when scheduled cases came in, keeping staff at the clinic until well beyond closing time at 6:00 p.m. This meant we had staff sitting around all day with little to do, yet who ended up being paid overtime—week after week. I realized if the satellite clinic was going to start making money, I needed to change that dynamic. But how?

I knew the staff were caring and good workers, and we occasionally had busy days that we cruised through, happily helping patients and their owners. So, the problem didn't lie with the staff themselves, but with the scheduling. We all knew the daily close-out figures (final income for the day) for our revenue but nothing more because my boss kept the financial details under wraps. I looked at the revenue produced on our busiest day and realized that if we could somehow manage to be that busy every day, then the business would be successful.

So I created a three-month challenge for the staff. I picked the revenue amount of our best day ever (a figure I knew was possible because we had met it once) and told the staff that, for the duration of the challenge, I would buy a candy bar for each staff member who worked on any day that we met or exceeded that amount of revenue. It was a stretch, since we had only made that amount once before. As a further stretch goal, I told them that if we met that goal for a week, I'd treat everyone to a pizza party.

Well, we never did have a pizza party, but the candy bars started coming out a few times each month. And even when we didn't meet that arbitrary revenue goal, we managed to book more clients overall and increased our average revenue. How did we achieve that? What had changed?

First, I got the staff involved. While a candy bar seemed like a tiny incentive, it was more than that. The fact was that I included the staff, giving them a very concrete goal they had some stake in. Once they had a reason to care how many clients were booked each day, they started to pay attention to those figures and actively work toward increasing them rather than simply going about their usual jobs. I noticed that when a client called to book an appointment, there was no longer a tendency among the staff to book it on another day. Instead, the staff would try and fit the client in as soon as possible, stacking the schedule rather than spacing it out, to ensure we got to our revenue goal. Interestingly, although the challenge lasted just three months, employees who had been part of it would still proudly tell me about the busy days they had—many years later!

Even after the sweet-tooth incentive was removed, the change in mindset and increased sense of agency among the staff remained. The workday was full, staff didn't have to stay to work overtime, and the staff morale improved as they were using their talents to help more pets each day. Not surprisingly, the clinic began to turn around, and closing it down no longer seemed like a good option.

With the engaged staff, additional workflow changes were welcomed and implemented quickly. The culture remained positive, and clients noticed, referring their friends to the clinic and eventually making the business flourish. The satellite clinic continued to grow, ultimately becoming so successful that it carried the main clinic through the 2008 economic slowdown, a complete turnaround in my boss's expectations for that business.

My experience with figuring out how to stack the formerly sluggish schedule at the satellite clinic taught me that I was able to assess and diagnose problems in business the same way I could with my patients. In this instance, I'd been able to diagnose that the issue with the satellite clinic lay in the subjective mindset of the staff members who had gotten used to the relaxed pace of scheduling clients "later" just as much as in the objective facts and figures reflecting its success or failure. Over the years since this experience, as I've refined that realization and practiced it on different business models, I've found that this analytical pattern of thinking can easily be taught and used by anyone looking to "vet" their own business!

AN ACADEMIC APPLICATION

Veterinarians tend to be driven, and I was no exception. I volunteered my time on local professional veterinary boards and supported our local animal shelters and health department by participating in free vaccination clinics. So it was an easy "yes" when I was asked to create a small presentation for a fundraiser, an education event called the Mini-Vet School, for the local pet emergency charity run by one of those local veterinary boards. Although I had never taught or presented other than for class projects in school, I loved veterinary medicine and supported the cause of this fundraiser, so I was willing to struggle through learning the technology to create a forty-five-minute lesson for the public who chose to attend. About two hundred local animal lovers signed up to be the "students" for that four-night event, and eight veterinarians volunteered to be the "instructors." These "students" seemed to enjoy the session with my topic—elderly cat diseases and issues—and asked a lot of questions. I had a lot of fun and enjoyed the intellectual curiosity of these animal lovers.

I was surprised to be approached shortly after that presentation by a professor from the local college. She had enjoyed my presentation and thought I might be interested in part-time teaching in the local veterinary technology program, training the veterinary technicians—vet techs—who are essentially the nurses of the veterinary profession. Always up for a challenge, I added teaching to my calendar, at first part-time, then full-time, and eventually I became a tenured professor.

Meanwhile, I continued to practice veterinary medicine part-time, loving my patients and long-term clients, but I found I truly enjoyed supporting the entire profession by training these dedicated students as they prepared for the rigorous national licensing exam and then graduated into a career they loved.

A few years into teaching, the department chair went on sabbatical, and I was tapped to lead the department in his absence. I was suddenly plunged into the "business" of academia. Could I apply the same techniques I'd used to revamp veterinary businesses?

The veterinary technology program had animals on campus for the students to learn with (and later adopt into their homes when class was over). Students learned by working with these animals in labs that simulated actual veterinary practice, learning physical examination, medical procedures, anesthesia, and surgical assisting. At the end of the school year, these animals received a free spay or neuter to become adoptable, so they could find a loving home (often that home would be with one of the students!). The department included professors and teachers but also support staff to care for these animals and to supervise the students. There was a budget to follow and a national accrediting organization whose guidelines had to be carefully implemented and monitored.

Although I had no previous knowledge of academic administration, I found the S.O.A.P. concept worked as well for academia as it had for small business. I went about identifying subjective and objective data into a problem list, assessing the problems, and coming up with a plan.

The subjective aspect included how students felt about their classes and teachers and how the staff and professors felt about each other, the administration, the students, the schedule, etc. Objective data included academic assessments (such as student recruitment and retention, class size, and student performance on the national accreditation exam) as well as budgeting financials (tuition income and program spending). I used the assessment aspect to organize my thoughts in this new academic arena, helping me to make sense of a new management entity while still being effective by creating a pertinent plan for any problems I could identify.

One of my first assessments revealed that I needed additional training in running a team. My previous management experience had been with a small team that I also worked with day-to-day, but this academic department included members I might only see at weekly or monthly meetings. Among staff, I sensed some interpersonal issues percolating that I knew could escalate to drama and upset, which I identified in the "subjective" list. Perhaps because I was in academia at the time, it was easy for me to step back and recognize that I needed to obtain more knowledge about how to manage a larger team if I wanted to be effective in handling these issues. The S.O.A.P. methodology helped me identify what needed to be done, even if I—the manager doing the assessing—was part of the plan!

If you think of your business like an animal patient, management is one of the "body systems" that needs to be addressed. Management needs to grow as the business grows or as the position changes. In this case, I needed to work on my knowledge of how to handle interpersonal issues on this larger team than I had previously managed, and my analysis helped me see that need clearly, which led me to seek out and complete the training required to handle this next level.

Boosted by my increased understanding of team dynamics and by a team that responded well to our initiatives, my time as the acting chair passed uneventfully and drama-free. Apparently, that was greatly appreciated, as I was tapped to become program manager for the main associate's degree program when the department chair returned. Identifying the potential interpersonal issues and implementing the plan to train myself to prevent and manage them helped the program run smoothly and moved me to a further leadership role.

TAKEAWAYS

- S.O.A.P. is an **effective methodology for diagnosing problems at an underperforming business**.

- Collating disparate elements such as employee complaints and financial challenges into a cohesive **problem list allows you to prioritize those problems**, similar to triage in the medical field.

- The **assessment** phase is critical to determining underlying issues, analyzing their impact, and determining a plan for addressing the problems identified.

- The **plan** is created as a working document that will inform action steps and guide subsequent S.O.A.P. follow-up analysis.

4

STOP THE BLEEDING

In veterinary medicine, the full S.O.A.P. system may be modified in an emergency situation where time is of the essence. If the patient has life-threatening injuries, there isn't time to carefully examine and assess all the possible issues. Instead, the veterinarian quickly checks for the critical systems using ABC: Airway, Breathing, Cardiovascular.

If the patient isn't breathing or the heart isn't pumping blood correctly, the other problems don't matter, and the doctor immediately acts to correct these life-threatening issues. After the patient's life is saved, we can then go through the formal S.O.A.P., but until then, those other problems don't matter—and looking for them can even slow down the important work of saving a life.

Business entities can also have emergencies—situations and legal troubles that threaten financial health, brand reputation, and so on. If an emergency situation is identified, the main focus should be on correcting this situation, and the finer details can wait until the emergency is successfully handled. In these cases, an abbreviated S.O.A.P. can be used; rather than carefully assessing all areas of the business, focus solely on the emergency and any related problems in the assessment and plan.

In this chapter, I describe how I used S.O.A.P. to unravel a mystery and solve a vexing financial issue.

A NEW CHALLENGE

After a few years of managing the veterinary technology degree program, I began receiving recruiting offers from other veterinary technology colleges around the country that wanted me to take over their programs. It was exciting to visit these programs and see how I could help them grow and improve. One offer was too good to ignore, and I informed the owner of the veterinary practice where I still worked part-time that I would likely accept this position and be leaving the area.

Learning of my interest in more complex management and new challenges, she made a counteroffer, hoping to keep me local and available to continue working for her part-time. She, along with most of the area's veterinary practice owners, was a shareholder of the local veterinary emergency clinic. The clinic just wasn't doing well, and the board of directors was looking for a full-time hospital administrator to take on oversight of this practice. They would match the other offer I had received. Would I be interested?

This was a compelling proposition. She didn't know that I already had a distinct fondness for this veterinary emergency clinic. I had raised a child as a single mother, working as a veterinarian by day, and the reason I could be home with my son at night and on weekends was that this emergency clinic handled the after-hours pet emergencies. Although my son was now grown and living in another state, I was still grateful that the emergency clinic had allowed me to be with him for so much of his childhood. My first year as a veterinarian had been in a community with no emergency clinic, and I had to either pay for expensive late-night childcare or take my then-toddler child along with me to handle emergencies with my patients. I was ecstatic when I moved to the community with this veterinary emergency facility so I didn't have to cover my own after-hours emergencies and could simply work my day job as a veterinarian.

Learning that the after-hours clinic wasn't doing well triggered my interest. While I knew little about veterinary emergency medicine, I was fairly confident that I could manage this new type of veterinary business, and the challenge to discover and turn around a clinic that personally meant something to me was compelling. If I could help this emergency clinic, I would be helping a lot of other veterinarians go home to their families at night. I said yes.

When I first arrived at the veterinary emergency clinic, I was excited to dig into my new role as hospital administrator. Once again, I found myself in the position to manage a new type of business. I started with—you guessed it—a S.O.A.P. analysis. This proved extremely important to me as I made an initial assessment of this ailing business.

Subjectively, it appeared that many of the doctors and staff appeared resigned or disengaged and had no confidence that anyone in management could fix the business. Was this due to working nights and weekends, or was it something more? Objectively, the financials that the board of directors shared with me seemed appropriate and couldn't explain the lack of profit. I knew something wasn't right, but what was it?

The hospital used an accounting software that I wasn't familiar with, so I decided I needed to learn how to use it to make sense of the financial data. I made a "sandbox" for myself with this software and pulled the past few months of records to see if I could re-create the financials to test my use of the different software, but I just couldn't get the sandbox records to match the board of director reports. The expenses reported to the board of directors were much higher than the paid bills I found in the files, so we always came up short on overall net income. What was I missing?

AN UNWELCOME SURPRISE

Two weeks after I started that new position, the checking account statement came, and I opened it to find that we barely had enough money to cover payroll! This definitely counted as an emergency situation for the business. Reviewing my S.O.A.P. notes and creating a problem list didn't give me many answers to explain the shortage of available cash in the checking account. Demand for our services was good, revenue appeared to be strong, and expenses didn't seem unreasonable. But I was handicapped by having no benchmarks for emergency hospital expenses. At the time, most financial analysis in the industry was focused on the typical small-animal general practice model and I couldn't find KPIs for emergency or specialty practice types. However, nothing was glaringly obvious at first glance. Naturally, my action plan needed to involve a deeper dive into the financials.

I noticed that a couple of employees had used personal credit cards for business expenses, which were later reimbursed to them. Learning that the business didn't have its own credit card, I reviewed these expenses to see what was being purchased and who should get the company card I planned to obtain. All of the receipts were readily available—except for the top manager's.

When I asked this man, the hospital director, for the receipts, he instantly broke into a very long, involved, and patently untrue discussion about how all his credit card receipts were with his accountant. His tall tales had the hair on the back of my neck standing up. I could tell he was lying. And his credit card was used monthly for rather large, unexplained amounts. I could feel my heart rate increasing as I struggled to remain calm.

If he was lying about getting me these receipts, and he had been the director for the past fifteen years, I remember thinking I may have just found the reason the business had not been making a profit. I pulled myself together enough to pretend that I accepted his explanation. Not sure how to proceed, I chose to act as if I believed his story and told him to get me the receipts as soon as he got them back from his accountant.

Since this clinic had been in place for a long time, and this director had been in the top position for years, I was very concerned about the potential for financial impropriety that could be serious and long-term. I also didn't know if he had any accomplices. Suddenly, my S.O.A.P. evaluation had turned into an emergency action plan with one clear first step: I needed to seek legal advice.

The lawyer suggested I tell no one at the clinic, not even the board of directors, that I suspected financial impropriety. Instead, I should get in touch with a local district attorney (DA). When speaking with the DA, I learned that life isn't quite like a TV crime drama. The DA's main job was to prosecute, not investigate. Her office couldn't perform any investigation without very solid evidence of wrongdoing, and that had to be obtained by the business itself. Given that I was the only one with this suspicion, and because so many shareholders were friends of the long-term hospital director, this meant that I was suddenly a part of my own business action plan. The DA was willing to coach me on what to look for and help me get financial record access, but they couldn't come on the premises of a private business. Suddenly, my new plan included an undercover investigation!

LAUNCHING A BUSINESS ACTION PLAN

I decided to dig a little deeper. I discovered that key financial records were missing, and the hospital director had inappropriate cash controls and financial management practices in place. That gave me immediate fodder for my problem list. I soon found out that I had to rely extensively on S.O.A.P. to keep me running the business while I conducted my covert investigation of the director and his credit card expenses. My mind was taken up with the undercover investigation, but I had to continue to move the business forward. The S.O.A.P. method helped me continue to manage enough day-to-day processes to keep the business running while hiding the fact that a lot of my time was being spent secretly investigating.

My S.O.A.P. review had identified issues that frustrated the staff, such as running out of important inventory items or not keeping important equipment maintained. I used my problem list to address some of these obvious issues one by one, so it was clear to staff that I was paying attention and helping improve our operations. As long as I kept fixing a problem or two like this every week or so, it seemed plausible that was all I was doing, so the hospital director had no suspicion I was also reviewing the financials and monitoring his activities.

At the time (before we turned this into a 24/7/365 clinic), the hospital only saw emergency patients overnight and on weekends, while the administrative staff usually worked Monday through Friday during the day and didn't really overlap with the medical staff. By appearing to focus only on medical operations rather than administrative issues, it made sense that many of my hours at the hospital would be in the evenings and on weekends, when the hospital director usually didn't work. In this manner, I was able to review historical records and identify financial issues without the knowledge of any administrative staff. The S.O.A.P. analysis provided me with enough obvious operational issues to fix that it looked like I was busy focusing on those problems, and this provided me with perfect cover for my covert activities—finding the evidence of wrongdoing.

KEEPING MY COVER WHILE INVESTIGATING

During my investigation, I identified a large number of problems with the financials but had to keep the hospital director from knowing he was under suspicion. At the same time, I needed to stop the ongoing losses by tightening the financial controls without tipping him off that I had discovered anything unusual. I was helped by the arrogance of the embezzler. He had fooled the shareholders for many years and was feeling invincible. I was able to appear slightly clueless about financials, which he believed, but I put in place normal financial controls, calling them "best practices," so he couldn't continue his behavior.

For example, I was able to keep the director from having access to the new company credit card by tying the issuance of the card to his missing receipts, saying I couldn't give him a company card until I was sure he could be counted on to provide receipts in a timely fashion. By focusing on the missing receipts as a matter of documentation rather than a suspicion of wrongdoing, I came across as a slightly clueless nitpicker. Thankfully, he had no idea I had any serious concerns.

I was able to work with the fraud department of the company's bank and found enough questionable material that the DA's office was willing to secretly subpoena the financial records for the director's credit card, where we matched the amounts reimbursed to him on that card with personal expenses, including several that he was also keeping hidden from his wife.

THE TURNAROUND

I was now managing a dual role of running the clinic while secretly investigating and collecting evidence of serious and chronic embezzlement by this director. I relied on the S.O.A.P. format to keep the regular business functioning well, but my ranking of the problems was based on identifying and halting business processes that were under the control of this director or were inappropriate.

As an example, I knew that good cash control meant different employees received cash, reconciled the daily deposits, created the bank deposits, used the bank account, and checked the bank statements. In this case, there were only two individuals involved in cash handling, and most of it was under the control of this one hospital director. Hiring an outside accountant and performing some of the functions myself helped to stop that poor business practice and keep cash from disappearing. I likened that to stopping the bleeding of an emergency patient. I still had a lot to figure out, but at least I had stopped the ongoing loss!

It took six months for me to find enough proof of embezzlement for the DA to be willing to charge the hospital director with Class C felony embezzlement. While his arrest was satisfying, so was the much-improved financial situation of the emergency clinic. Just putting the normal financial practices in place and halting the ongoing embezzlement created a complete financial turnaround. For the first time in years, we had enough profit to upgrade our medical equipment and improve working conditions for the doctors and staff. The local veterinary hospital owners who were shareholders finally started seeing a return on their investment in the community veterinary emergency facility.

As an interesting side note, the hospital director made a plea deal by paying back some of the funds identified as embezzled and getting the charge reduced to a Class D felony, and this development hit the local news. After it became public knowledge, I was informed by someone in the veterinary community that the manager had previously worked in a veterinary hospital in a different city and had been fired for embezzling a small amount. That veterinarian hadn't pursued the issue beyond firing him, and he had simply taken his knowledge of embezzling to the next clinic. He needed to be stopped, and I'm glad we stopped him.

INVESTIGATE AND ANALYZE

I won't go so far as to say that the S.O.A.P. format was the reason I could get an embezzler stopped, but it certainly helped keep me on track as I tried to balance running the business with handling an undercover investigation on that same business. It was similar to a veterinarian handling a patient with multiple illnesses: S.O.A.P. can help identify critical action steps and keep priorities straight so you can achieve the best outcome. In this case, the practice started making a profit as soon as the cash controls and good business practices were put in place, even during the six months that the hospital director was still employed prior to his arrest. The S.O.A.P. analysis and action plan would have improved the business even if the embezzler had not been identified, simply by correcting obvious issues in financial practices.

It helped me focus on all the operational problems I had identified with S.O.A.P., even when I was secretly concerned with the financial improprieties. When my brain was trying to learn how to investigate a financial crime, S.O.A.P. kept me on track with the typical issues for running a business. Clients still needed to be served, and employees still needed to be paid. To keep me from becoming distracted, I created a S.O.A.P. analysis for different topics. Obviously, the financial investigation was its own S.O.A.P., but I also had to evaluate the normal business operations.

I used different aspects of the profit-and-loss statement to create areas to investigate and analyze. As an example, I broke down the business's expenses by categories and reviewed each separately: facilities, equipment, inventory, personnel, administrative, etc. I hadn't needed to do that before, when managing a smaller veterinary practice, but this practice was larger, and my simpler S.O.A.P. process had started to become overwhelming.

Some of my analyses would overlap, for instance, when I reviewed staffing and personnel, as these included expenses (e.g., payroll, benefits), which I had also analyzed in the financial S.O.A.P. There were subjective and objective measures that weren't simply financial, so I found it useful to categorize the different areas even if they overlapped.

For example, when payroll expenses seemed high, I might find there was a subjective component such as staff calling out sick more often due to burnout or unhappiness, resulting in more overtime for the remaining staff who had to cover those shifts. Having a S.O.A.P. in place for personnel helped me see the patterns and informed my financial S.O.A.P. action plan.

THE PARETO PRINCIPLE—80/20

During this overwhelming time, I also needed to develop a system to prioritize the issues I had identified in the S.O.A.P. notes, so I could triage them appropriately. At one point, I had asked my previous employer how she prioritized the issues of running her clinic, but when she told me that she simply stayed at work that day until everything was handled, I realized that she didn't understand the scope of the issues found in a larger business. I had to come to grips with that as well. There just wasn't time in the day to discover—let alone handle—all the possible issues!

I fell back on the 80/20 concept, also called the Pareto Principle, which essentially states that 80 percent of consequences come from 20 percent of causes. While it isn't an exact rule, I had previously found it does help identify the important areas of a business. When running the satellite veterinary clinic, I had determined that 20 percent of the clients produced a large portion of the revenue. After discovering that, I put in place some ways to give those particular clients extra recognition and value— for example, by ensuring all staff members knew the names and details of their pets so they could greet them personally without needing to access a file first—and was rewarded with their client loyalty and increase in revenue.

Applying this principle to my S.O.A.P. analyses, I began looking for the changes that would produce the biggest impact. This helped me stop the bleeding of finances faster. This was why one of my first actions was to implement normal cash controls. This fairly small and quick change made a huge impact, obviously, by removing the lack of oversight that allowed cash to disappear without a trace.

As an example, I divided the tasks of reconciling the daily receipts, making the bank deposit, and balancing the bank statement among the three administrative employees—myself, the hospital director, and the bookkeeper—with a report going to the board of directors each month. The second financial change I implemented was to immediately stop the practice of having employees reimbursed personally for business expenses they had incurred. Now they had to have those expenses paid by the new company credit card (that I controlled) with pre-approval for the expense.

Another change was to correct the way petty cash was handled. I was appalled to discover that petty cash consisted of a drawer in the bookkeeper's office with a big pile of loose bills and no record-keeping. The hospital director had set up a policy that much of the cash received was to be dropped into this drawer rather than deposited into the bank account. His reasoning for this practice was that vendors and maintenance personnel had to be paid cash out of this drawer because there was no company credit card.

Obviously, this meant there was no true tracking of where the cash went, and it was very easy for cash to disappear with no trace. I used the new company credit card as an excuse to change the entire petty cash procedure, stipulating that we must now pay vendors with a credit card and not cash.

Then I sat down with the bookkeeper, and the two of us counted all the cash in the drawer so we together witnessed the amount of cash piled in that drawer. I then deposited all but $20 into our bank account and required a log to be kept for any disbursement of the $20 petty cash. There was an uproar when I did this, with an insistence that we wouldn't be able to handle our business needs without this ready cash, but I remained adamant.

Interestingly, it turned out that we never needed to dip into the $20 of petty cash once the log was required, and none of the vendors or maintenance personnel objected to being paid either by credit card or by check. Our net monthly revenue and bank balance jumped when these financial best practices were instituted, further supporting the idea that there had previously been serious financial improprieties. I had correctly determined that a large improvement to the business could be made by the one simple step of instituting normal cash controls.

This entire revision showed me the importance of the analysis portion of the S.O.A.P. process. When the business is small, identifying the problems is a fairly quick process, and the fix may be just as obvious. When the business is larger, capturing all the problems is one important task, but it is equally as important to analyze *which* problems need to be dealt with first. Applying the 80/20 principle allows you to see what actions will make the biggest difference. I learned that I needed to block off thinking time to review, analyze, and strategize. Without this analysis and strategy, I could have spent all my time busy with many small tasks but with no real, long-term positive effect.

USING S.O.A.P. FOR PROJECT MANAGEMENT

Veterinary teams are resilient and dedicated, and the team at this emergency clinic was no exception. Once the serious business threat to the emergency clinic was resolved, the doctors and staff blossomed. They believed in their mission, and when they weren't being undermined by poor management, their hard work caused the business to steadily grow.

Once we turned things around financially, the board of directors resurrected their dream of turning the after-hours clinic into a 24/7/365 veterinary emergency hospital. My next project was to transform a clinic that was focused on stabilizing emergencies and transferring patients to their regular veterinarians for care during normal business hours into a full-service emergency hospital. This required strategic planning and project management, and it was the first time I used the S.O.A.P. methodology to identify what needed to be done for a future project. I found that the problem-oriented S.O.A.P. process worked extremely well for planning purposes. I went through the familiar S.O.A.P. steps to get the project organized.

- **S:** First, the subjective: How would this affect our clients? Our referring veterinarians? Our reputation? Our doctors and staff?

- **O:** Then, the objective: What staffing, facilities, equipment, medical records, and medication changes would be needed to make this jump?

- **A:** Armed with answers to these questions, I assessed each identified problem.

- **P:** And I wrote up an action plan for the project.

One of the issues was that this idea had been floated around for over a decade and had never come to fruition, so there was a lot of inertia pulling for this to be yet another failed attempt. On the other hand, I was riding a wave of positivity as their leader from having found and fixed the embezzlement issue. I decided that bold action was needed, and I announced a date, just five months in the future, when we would go 24/7. The timeline was so soon that it was terrifying (though I didn't let anyone know my trepidation), but it also wouldn't leave any time for a pause or delay that might let everyone sink back into resignation or resistance.

I used the team management skills I had learned in my roles at the veterinary technology college and shared the plan, delegating portions and including ideas to get everyone excited. There was no time to stop, and I leaned on my constantly updated S.O.A.P. plans to monitor and move the project forward. On Memorial Day weekend that year, we worked through the long weekend as usual but then did not close the next weekday morning, breaking the operational pattern that had been in place for over thirty-five years. We were now 24/7/365!

By now, I realized that careful analysis and planning could move a wide variety of initiatives forward. I used the S.O.A.P. methodology for quick analysis of day-to-day issues as well as long-term projects. With careful preparation and an excited and committed team in place, the 24/7 hospital continued to grow and be successful. When I received an unexpected call to apply for a new position, I knew that the emergency clinic was almost running itself, so I was open to the next challenge.

TAKEAWAYS

- During times of emergency at your organization, just like with a real-life patient, your main focus should be **treating the problem until the emergency is handled**. Skip straight to evaluating the emergency and any related problems in the assessment and plan.

- While the emergency is ongoing, use S.O.A.P. to **keep you on track as you balance overseeing day-to-day business operations with handling the emergency**. S.O.A.P. can help you identify critical action steps and keep your priorities straight.

- The **Pareto Principle states that 80 percent of consequences come from 20 percent of causes**. Use this to inform your S.O.A.P. analyses, especially when you are strained by emergency circumstances.

- The problem-oriented S.O.A.P. methodology **can also be used proactively for project management** to determine a future goal and plan the action steps needed for successful implementation.

5

A NONPROFIT APPLICATION

One chilly night in late November, I was backing out of a parking space, eager to drive home, when my car's Bluetooth indicated I was receiving a phone call. I automatically answered, expecting a sales call or a quick question from my team. I was surprised when the caller identified himself as a faculty member at a veterinary college in the Midwest, who was heading up a search committee to find their next director of hospital operations. My name had come up as a good potential candidate for the job, based on national recognition I had received in an industry magazine, *DVM360*. I was also recently a top-ten finalist for Practice Manager of the Year by the Veterinary Hospital Managers Association.

There are only about thirty veterinary schools that have teaching hospitals associated with the colleges, and this was one of them. While some veterinary schools send their students out to working veterinary practices for training, these powerhouse veterinary colleges run their own hospitals, which provide both routine and specialty care while teaching the next generation of veterinarians. They can also help further research and new technologies.

I carefully pulled my car back into the parking space, trying to wrap my head around this. Someone was calling me from another state and considering me for such a prestigious position to oversee all their teaching hospitals. We spoke for almost an hour, and they told me about the open position, painting a word picture of the college and region that had me intrigued.

After the call, I drove home and told my husband all about our conversation. The college was well respected, and although I'd naturally heard of it, I did some internet research anyway. I learned that, at the time, most of the higher-level management at this college was male, and almost all had Midwestern roots. Knowing how academic search committees worked from my time as a local faculty member, I concluded they probably had an in-house candidate in mind. But they'd have to interview at least three candidates as a show of good faith, and it would look good to interview a female candidate.

I figured that was the end of it, but a few days later, the acting dean of the veterinary school called me when I was at home. This time, I put the call on speaker so my husband could hear our conversation. The dean knew about my history of turning around veterinary businesses. He was seeking a director to improve the financial picture of the teaching hospitals, someone who understood the nuances of academia as opposed to just coming from a for-profit business background. But they wanted to make sure they chose a candidate who could still balance the teaching needs with financial health. He directly asked me to apply for the position.

After the call, my husband and I pondered the opportunity. We had been married only five years, and he had never lived anywhere else. But when he heard that there were only thirty veterinary colleges with teaching hospitals, my sports-loving husband likened it to being asked to coach an NFL team: It was a position you just didn't refuse! I still figured they didn't really want me, but I thought it could be fun to go through the interview process, so I applied.

To my surprise, my application was accepted, and a phone interview was set up shortly afterward. This was a phone interview with nine members of the search committee. I managed to get their names beforehand so I could look them up on the website to get an idea of their roles at the college.

During the phone interview, I leaned on my S.O.A.P. fundamentals, asking them as many questions as they asked of me. I was curious about how their hospitals worked and asked questions about key subjective and objective aspects of a business and how those aspects were expressed at that college. I suspected I'd never have a better chance to learn about veterinary teaching hospitals. I didn't really look at the opportunity as much more than that, since I still figured they were interviewing me simply to "check a box" on the number of interviewees they needed to meet with.

But I was in for a further surprise. It turned out that my insightful questions during the interview had indicated to the search committee that I really knew how a veterinary academic institution worked and that I would be able to figure out whatever I didn't know. They now wanted to fly my husband and me to the area to show us around and have me interview in person. The interview would be held over two days, and they wanted to know my vision for their hospital as the main focus.

I now kicked my S.O.A.P. analysis into high gear. The search committee's answers to my questions had been a starting point, and I knew I now needed to dive into approaching the teaching hospitals like I would any business I wanted to analyze. Because it was a public institution, there was a fair amount of information available online.

WORKING S.O.A.P. FROM THE OUTSIDE IN

I started applying my S.O.A.P. methodology to the teaching hospitals in earnest during this period, starting at the beginning with subjective data. I researched the college personnel directory to get an idea of the people working there. I was very impressed not only with the credentials of the veterinary teaching faculty but also with the high quality of the veterinary technicians working as hospital support staff. I searched social media, discovering that there was a lot of room for improvement there with respect to visibility. Reviews seemed positive, indicating that clients were happy with the services, but there was little online presence or client-facing information about the great work performed by the hospitals.

Then for objective data, I found that there was not much publicly available financial data, but I could look at the operational setup. I reviewed what specialties and departments were available and where the different veterinary teaching hospitals were located in the state. I reviewed the cost of living in the area and got an idea of the client demographics.

As best as I could, I pulled together an analytical review of what I found. Then, I came up with a plan for each of the issues I had identified. I ensured that plan was tied to the mission and vision of the college and teaching hospital. I created a PowerPoint with this information and presented it to the search committee and other interested parties during the in-person interview.

In retrospect, my incorrect assumption that they had an internal candidate and weren't really considering me for the position had worked in my favor. I was relaxed during the interview and spent my time over the two-day period getting to know the people rather than trying to impress them. I really had fun learning how the institution worked. I went home after the interview, happy that my husband and I had a nice tour and learned about a great college, but I had no further expectations. I was, therefore, shocked when I quickly received an offer of employment.

By this time, the emergency hospital that I oversaw—the one now running 24/7/365—was running smoothly, and it didn't seem to need me at all. I had a good team in place, and I felt that they didn't really need me either. I was excited about the challenge of overseeing multiple hospitals and making a difference in a college that trained future veterinarians. I accepted the offer with my husband's support, and off we went on an adventure in the Midwest—one that was to last almost four years.

SCALING UP THE STRATEGY

Right away, I found that everyone at the college was kind and helpful. They readily answered any of my questions as I began my more formal S.O.A.P., now using real information, not just what I had gleaned from website searches. Within a couple of days, the S.O.A.P. information I'd collected was immense and unwieldy. The scale of this operation was so much more than I had dealt with before.

My first action step was to recognize that I needed to step up my delegation game immediately and lean on others to fulfill key roles. I also realized that very few management systems were already in place that were suitable for an operation of this size. It was as if this huge institution were being managed with the same tools I had used when running that first small satellite clinic. A strategic overhaul was needed right away.

I was now part of an internal cabinet that reported directly to the dean of the veterinary school. The cabinet was responsible for reporting on the function of the teaching hospitals on a biweekly basis. I also met quarterly with the university provost, essentially the chief financial officer of all the colleges in the university system. During this meeting, I'd give a financial report on affiliated hospitals that weren't directly part of the teaching hospital system.

As I organized my strategy, I had to keep conflicting interests in mind, as there were many different factors to juggle, which was clear just from reviewing the existing mission of the teaching hospitals—excellence in teaching and patient care, as would be expected, but also so much more.

The teaching aspect consisted of training the veterinary students who rotated through the different departments in the hospitals during their final year of veterinary school, their last chance to learn prior to graduating and practicing veterinary medicine on their own. During this point of their career, the students required foundational lessons and careful monitoring by the teaching faculty, as they were working on client-owned pets (called small-animal medicine) and livestock (called large-animal medicine), learning how to treat both small and large animal species.

At the same time, the veterinary college was also where already-licensed veterinarians came to learn advanced veterinary techniques as part of continued specialty training. Veterinary colleges with teaching hospitals are also referral centers, and in some cases, they are the last resort for patients with complex medical issues that require advanced or novel treatments by highly trained specialists. Thus, research was part of that mission, as new treatments and procedures needed to be developed and tested, and veterinarians seeking to become the next generation of specialists required these complex cases to learn from.

Teaching these foundational and complex veterinary techniques fell to a relatively small number of highly respected veterinary faculty members, who balanced teaching with their demanding caseload of patient care duties. While the teaching aspect of their work in the hospital was subsidized by their general faculty salaries paid by the university, it was expected that the veterinary teaching hospitals pay for the overall operations as well, including the small salaries of the interns and residents (house officers) as they learned to become specialists, the salaries of the support staff, and the general medical equipment and medications. So, even though this academic teaching institution was nonprofit, it still needed to be financially stable.

Strategic Action Versus Crisis Management

There were multiple hospitals and programs to be supervised from my position. My analysis was now strategic and big-picture, but the S.O.A.P. technique still worked. The difference was that with this larger business entity, I now used zones or areas and identified action plans for each area. I then trained and empowered a team of middle managers in the different units to take the action steps.

The S.O.A.P. plan worked to clarify the plan and manage the delegated actions with the management team. It also helped me remain aware of the strategic goals in a position that was virtually swamped with various urgent issues, which I jokingly referred to as "the crisis du jour." One upper-management danger is being consumed by handling these daily crises and forgetting the overall strategic goals. I kept the action steps on a spreadsheet and reviewed them weekly with the appropriate managers, giving them support as needed.

I soon learned to block off time in my weekly schedule to privately review the week and "true up" my actions with the strategic goals. It was sometimes difficult to pull myself away from crisis management, but I discovered that any week where I skipped this step, I ended up being less productive. I justified this fall in productivity by telling myself that I was busy handling lots of urgent issues that always cropped up and couldn't be ignored, which was often true, but I found that the mission of the veterinary college was better served when I kept my actions in line with the strategic goals.

When I went away on a vacation, I learned an excellent lesson in the importance of focusing on the strategic goals found through my S.O.A.P. analysis rather than constantly handling urgent issues that constantly seemed to need my attention. Typically, during my time "off," I would still respond to emails, phone calls, or text messages to support my team. However, on this vacation, I would be off-grid and unable to communicate.

After ten days, I returned to find a slew of emails and text messages—just as I'd feared. But then I noticed something interesting. The urgent crises that had occurred earlier during my vacation had generally been dealt with later in the week. When they got my "away" message or simply didn't get a response from me, solutions were found anyway!

This helped me realize that by jumping in quickly to personally deal with every "crisis du jour," I was stifling the creativity of my team. I was still acting as a day-to-day manager rather than a director of the overall system. From that time on, I added a technique of benign neglect to the urgent issues, waiting a bit to allow others to find solutions and stepping in only when my guidance was truly needed. Now, I could actually spend the time needed to further my long-term goals and strategies for the whole institution, moving new initiatives and addressing systemic issues.

Learning to Apply Different Financial Criteria

My initial strategic analysis recognized a major inherent conflict affecting my ability to improve the financial well-being of these nonprofit teaching hospitals: A well-run veterinary business would typically achieve financial stability by balancing client demand and operational costs with pricing and the number of patient cases seen, allowing for a return on investment by the owners.

However, this veterinary college was part of a state-owned institution, meaning that essentially, the taxpayers were the true owners, and the return on their investment was to have access to reasonably priced, excellent veterinary care. Pricing was strictly controlled and not easily subject to change. Caseload was limited as well due to the demands of effective student teaching.

Unlike the veterinary school, a typical private practice veterinary caseload would not allow students to take the time needed to learn about each patient, which would often be their first exposure to a disease or condition. But here at the teaching hospitals, each case provided a learning opportunity, meaning it took time. Increasing the caseload would decrease the teaching time for each case, as only the faculty members had the knowledge and experience to process cases quickly. This would result in the students being left as observers, which is not the best method for learning. I was restricted from increasing caseload by these considerations.

So, if I couldn't improve the financial picture by increasing prices or increasing patient caseload, what was left? I pursued two options. First, there was the amazing generosity of members of the public who were willing to donate money to support the teaching and research functions of the veterinary college. This had not been an option in private practice, and I was moved by the deep dedication of these donors. I noticed that there was no funding group for the overall operations of the hospital, so I worked with the appropriate college personnel to create such a fund, providing the opening donation myself. While small, this fund was intended to grow and help with the "behind-the-scenes" operational costs typically handled by reinvesting profit into a business. Second, I leaned on improving efficiency. Almost every business can become more efficient, and the teaching hospital was no exception. For this, I went back to my S.O.A.P. analysis.

HOW TO HANDLE TOO MANY PROBLEMS

I had spent the first several weeks at my new position walking around the different hospitals, meeting the faculty, house officers, and staff. In the process, I collected dozens of complaints from all of them about what wasn't working and many hopes and dreams about what could be possible. I then organized these in a huge spreadsheet that I could manipulate and got to work. I'd never had to use a spreadsheet for my S.O.A.P. analysis before, but there were just too many issues to capture any other way.

Using the spreadsheet, I organized the different issues into common categories, such as equipment, staffing, and facilities. By reviewing these complaints grouped together, I could spot trends and duplicate or even find competing requests. I also rated each issue by importance to the overall mission and gave them a simple action timeframe, using those ratings to give a triage weight to each problem. I highlighted the most urgent in red so I could see them quickly. With my priorities sorted, I started the lengthy process of addressing all these issues over time.

Obviously, I couldn't correct all the individual issues in several hospitals all by myself, which is why my first action was to work on the overall administrative structure to organize a management team. This meant creating new supervisory positions throughout the hospitals, promoting or hiring appropriate personnel, and training these new leaders. My S.O.A.P. spreadsheet was a useful starting point for their training on the job. I could identify which issues would best fall under the purview of a new leader, delegate the group of tasks, and then let that supervisor go to work, connecting with them weekly to give support and coaching or working with them to get needed resources.

My spreadsheet gained new tabs as I moved tasks to a separate page for each new supervisor. Sure enough, issues began to be resolved with the help of these dynamic individuals who were hungry for the opportunity to improve the function of the various hospitals.

As I released these operational duties to junior leaders, my time was freed up to analyze larger strategic issues. I had identified some potential opportunities for improvement during my assessment—new programs, new partnerships—but with so many operational issues needing to be handled, these strategic goals had been postponed or ignored for years. Returning to the patient analogy from the previous chapter, these operational issues were the bleeding that had to be stopped. But without a good organizational structure, there had never been time to move beyond remedying the continual operational crises.

I now had multiple S.O.A.P. documents, each divided by the different hospitals and which leader was tasked with handling the issues. I was able to pull the strategic issues into a special S.O.A.P. problem list for me to handle directly. Because I now had created and trained a strong middle-management team, I could spend my intellectual resources on improving systems and adding programs and partnerships. The combination of strong operational control and strategic thinking quickly improved the overall function of the different hospitals.

FAMILIAR TOOLS IN UNCERTAIN TIMES

One large, unexpected issue cropped up suddenly in March 2020, a date seared into the memory of most who lived through the COVID pandemic, just as the new organizational system really started showing huge improvements. The global pandemic brought our familiar operations to a screeching halt, and suddenly, we were navigating completely unfamiliar territory.

The veterinary teaching hospitals were affected when students were sent home. How do you teach clinical veterinary medicine virtually? Is caring for animals essential work? How do you protect hundreds of essential workers—who must work in close quarters—from a disease we know almost nothing about? This was a crisis on a large scale, and one that changed day by day and, in some cases, hour by hour.

The COVID pandemic crisis derailed life as usual for most of the world, and veterinary operations were no exception. Veterinary teaching hospitals have a relatively small support staff because veterinary students are in the hospital, learning their profession as they care for patients. When the university sent all the students home for their safety, this resulted in two immediate problems for the teaching hospitals: Who would care for the patients, and how could the students learn when they weren't at the hospital?

I attempted to make sense of the pandemic as it continued to change daily. I returned to the basic S.O.A.P. process to capture the new issues presented by this crisis. I was helped by brilliant minds across the veterinary profession, who freely shared their ideas of how best to provide veterinary care with minimal risk of COVID spread. Fairly quickly, we determined that clients could no longer be allowed into the hospital as we tried to minimize person-to-person contact. Thus, curbside operations were born.

I was impressed by the openness of all our doctors and staff to this new way of interacting with clients, accepting patient drop-offs, and then having difficult conversations over the phone. As the pandemic continued beyond the first few days and most businesses had to close down, hospital operations shifted as well. Routine veterinary care was halted, and only care of livestock (our food supply) and true emergency patients would be seen. This was intensely upsetting to dedicated veterinary professionals who had spent their careers caring for patients with preventative medicine, catching issues before they rose to an emergency level.

My S.O.A.P. analysis pointed out a new subjective issue as the veterinary professionals began dealing with the mental health effects of no longer being able to prevent disease and only dealing, day after day, with animals in crisis. On top of that stress were the angry clients who just didn't understand the constraints, and the personal stress of all the veterinary essential workers who didn't know whether they were about to catch a deadly disease from their coworker or bring it home to their vulnerable families. Caring for mental health issues became an important addition to the plan so that the human side of the profession could be supported as they, in turn, cared for the animals with whom we share our lives.

The S.O.A.P. technique was invaluable to me here. The subjective side was obvious, with the fear and anxiety evidenced on all sides. People needed to feel safe and be supported to work in this situation with known and unknown dangers. The objective data, on the other hand, changed frequently with each new discovery about the virus and how to prevent or treat it. Based on this data—the S and O—new policies had to be decided, written, disseminated, and then put into play immediately.

The assessment phase felt constant. I remember one Thursday morning when I awoke to find a new guideline from the Centers for Disease Control (CDC), and I worked on quickly writing a new policy that morning. By 10:00 a.m., the CDC had updated that policy again with new information, and I had to scrap my morning's work and start over!

The S.O.A.P. technique helped me remember the human, subjective side when I might otherwise have simply focused on the objective data in my action plans.

Everyone Steps Up and Pitches In

I joked that if I hadn't had gray hair before, running a series of hospitals full of essential workers through a pandemic would have caused my hair color to change to gray anyway. However, the reality was that every person at the hospitals stepped up in ways that were previously inconceivable.

The doctors and staff who made up the hospital quickly demonstrated an absolutely incredible commitment and dedication as they completely upended their lives to figure out how to keep the hospital running. The veterinary faculty showed their brilliance by developing entirely new methods of teaching that would be effective via distance learning in record time, and the students restarted their studies virtually. The veterinarian house officers stepped in to support the emergency sections of the hospital, taking on grueling ninety-hour weekly rotation schedules to keep emergency operations open 24/7. The veterinary support staff from all the nonessential sections of the hospital that were closed down rearranged their lives to take night and weekend patient care shifts that were left open by the loss of the veterinary students.

Everyone was amazingly patient with the constant changes (to mask or not to mask, to meet in person or virtually, to follow policy A in the morning and then learn policy B by afternoon, etc.). My job was to keep the hospitals caring for agricultural animals and pets in dire need, support the faculty who still had to train future veterinarians virtually in ways never tried before, and keep everyone safe while we did this. Having S.O.A.P. as a tool to quickly analyze the subjective and objective aspects of these changes helped me rapidly develop and disseminate policies to remain true to our mission in the face of a global pandemic.

As an administrator, I was ordered to work from home for the first six weeks of the pandemic, and I relied deeply on daily reports from various faculty and staff supervisors to continue to manage from afar. It was an uncertain time, and I found myself constantly creating new procedures and policies based on the latest medical information from the CDC and other reliable sources. As soon as I was allowed back on site, I returned to find that most of the university was a ghost town, with the exception of the vital hub of the essential veterinary services at the teaching hospitals.

As the director of one of the very few groups of essential workers at the university, I found myself thrust into a role of reviewing the constantly changing information about COVID and updating the related procedures, such as what to do if someone tested positive, if they were exposed, if they had a sniffle but tested negative, what kind of cleaning was needed to prevent COVID spread, and so on. It was not what I had expected at all, but again, the logic of the S.O.A.P. process still helped to organize even this unfamiliar subject.

Over the next year, a new normal was reached. Mask usage and improved medical knowledge allowed the students to return to campus eventually, and most of the closed departments opened up again. The efficiencies we had started to work on prior to the pandemic turned out to be extremely useful as pandemic disruptions in medical supplies and available staffing strained the profession.

Once again, I used the S.O.A.P. technique to identify, prioritize, and resolve these various issues and return the veterinary teaching hospitals to an even greater level of functionality. I had done what I'd set out to do: Fulfill the request of the acting dean who had hired me to turn around the finances of the organization. For that, I credit the logic and efficiency of the S.O.A.P. technique. I'm proud to have increased revenue in the veterinary teaching hospital system by a huge 50 percent in my first three years as director—despite the disruption of the pandemic!

TAKEAWAYS

- S.O.A.P. isn't only a tool for evaluating an organization you already work in; it can also be a **valuable means of assessing the strengths and weaknesses of an organization you're considering joining.**

- As long as you consider the organization's vision and mission, **S.O.A.P. can be scaled up or down to serve institutions of varying sizes and complexities.**

- It's essential to use S.O.A.P. to **organize your priorities and delineate responsibilities between upper and middle management** to prevent recurring low-level crises from stifling the organization's overall growth and profitability.

- Using S.O.A.P. to identify issues allows you to **delegate them to middle management**, freeing you to focus your mental resources on strategy and growth.

- S.O.A.P. allows you to **plot opportunities for growth by offering a framework by which to track and maintain accountability for long-term goals.**

- S.O.A.P. allows you **to track and prioritize the issues within your organization, which affords your organization agility** during times of great stress and change.

- During times of uncertainty or radical change, **use S.O.A.P. to redefine priorities, capabilities, and pain points** that reflect your organization's new circumstances.

6

MATCHING LEADERSHIP
TO CULTURE

I had the pleasure of taking a seven-day vacation on a cruise ship two years in a row. The first cruise impressed me because the cruise ship employees all seemed to be truly happy and supremely attentive. As a cruise ship guest, I was left feeling that each employee loved their job and enjoyed our interactions, so I had an immensely positive view of my cruise experience.

My second cruise was in a beautiful locale, and the amenities on the second ship were comparable to my first cruise. However, my experience was very different. The employees all performed their job duties, but they often appeared angry, bored, or resentful. It felt like all the cruise ship guests, including me, were seen as an inconvenience by the service staff. I was left with a distaste for that second cruise line.

What separated the two experiences? The only real difference between my cruise vacations was the feeling I got as a customer. I identify this as the "culture" of the business. Culture can be difficult to describe and hard to quantify, so it is worth taking a deeper look at it. While I don't know what was really happening on those cruise ships, to my eye, there was a completely different culture evidenced by the behavior and attitude of the staff of those two different cruise lines.

While culture is sometimes shrugged off as something that just happens, good leadership can improve culture. Between my two cruise vacations, I suspect manager leadership was at least one crucial difference. On the first ship, it was not uncommon to see the service managers walking around the decks. On the other hand, on the second cruise, I don't recall seeing a manager at all.

Attentive managers can often identify potential issues before they flare up into real problems and may be able to fix problems in the moment. On the first cruise, the restaurant manager had asked me twice in one week about the service I received, and the housekeeping manager checked in once that week. We often saw ship officers walking around public areas at intervals, willing to stop and chat with the cruise guests. With that much attention to customer service, I was left feeling that I would have had recourse with a manager should there have been a problem. Of course, with that level of service, there were no problems at all.

Yet, on the second cruise, I don't recall seeing a manager or ship officer anywhere during the entire week we were traveling. Because attentive managers help keep the operations flowing smoothly, employees feel supported when they know they can easily reach their manager with questions or concerns.

AN UNEXPECTED RETURN

As the initial pandemic crisis started to ease into a new way of life with less need for constant analysis and new actions, I received a surprising text from my former veterinary boss about the 24/7 veterinary emergency clinic I had left in such great shape only three years before. She wrote that the emergency clinic needed me again and implored, "Don't sign a new contract; we will get you back!"

I informed the dean of my university of the text and then kept him informed as the emergency clinic's board of directors started making offers to recruit me back. The benefits at the university were good, and I didn't think I would want to leave, but then I was offered an ownership share in the emergency clinic. That offer was too good to pass up. I gave the university a six-month notice and agreed to return.

Naturally, I presumed the clinic would continue to be successful before I agreed to move away to support the veterinary teaching college and give back to my profession. Now, I was excited to return as a shareholder. I found myself surprisingly happy to return to the city I had spent twenty-five years in, and my husband was happy to return to the city of his birth.

CULTURE ISSUES AT THE EMERGENCY CLINIC!

Imagine the shock I felt on my return when I discovered there had been a complete negative turnaround in the culture of this emergency facility! Three and a half years before, I had left a thriving, happy clinic. What I found now was a clinic that had only a third of the previous number of veterinarians working and a serious deficit in the number of staff as well. The day I arrived, the two middle managers weren't there to greet me. They had not been able to take vacations for a year and were about to lose their accrued time off if they didn't. Assuming I'd know what to do, they had started their vacations the day I came!

The clinic was losing valuable staff almost daily, and those who remained felt demoralized and miserable. The explanations weren't difficult to find; the woman who replaced me had been fired after it had become clear that her management style relied on fear and intimidation, which obviously didn't work well in a veterinary setting.

The veterinary profession is unquestionably scientific, but the people who make up the profession have huge hearts. They could all find higher-paying jobs in other professions, including human healthcare, but they have a strong drive to care for animals. They do not need to be *scared* into doing their jobs. In fact, one of the biggest challenges in managing veterinary professionals is getting staff members to care for themselves and not burn out by spending too much of their time, heart, and effort on patients while ignoring their own needs. My predecessor's management method based on punishment and fear had only served to push hardworking employees away.

The board of directors eventually realized that this executive needed to go, and she was removed from the position. While that was a step forward, the board did not fill this position, so the remaining middle managers were expected to fill the gap—with no training in higher management. If life had continued as normal, even that could have been weathered, but then COVID happened. From my time at the veterinary teaching hospital during the pandemic, I knew that keeping an essential business running—while people were terrified and scientific recommendations and health laws were constantly changing—was an incredibly stressful task, even for a well-seasoned executive.

The remaining management team at the emergency clinic had done their best, but the combined issues were just too much; many employees decided they had no choice but to leave for better-managed veterinary practices.

Pushing Through the Stress of Fatigue

This exodus was exacerbated by the unfortunate fact that veterinary medicine is one of the caring professions that has a high risk of compassion fatigue. *Compassion fatigue* is the emotional exhaustion caused by exposure to a high level of serious issues eliciting a caring and compassionate reaction. It actually falls into the category of secondary traumatic stress. The veterinary profession has always been at risk of compassion fatigue by attracting very caring individuals who deeply believe in their work to provide healthcare for animals, but it was worsened during the time of the COVID pandemic, as I had seen at the veterinary teaching hospitals.

It is common knowledge that during the COVID pandemic, human healthcare workers had to deal with a tremendous amount of stress, based on the constant number of COVID patients who were sick and dying. It is less common knowledge that during the pandemic, other professions staffed with those considered essential workers also had increased stress. The veterinary profession was considered essential for the animal food supply and livestock care, but states had varying reactions to allowing veterinary care during the height of the pandemic. In some states, veterinarians were not allowed to treat pets for a time, which was not only devastating for the pet owners but also deeply upsetting to the veterinary professionals.

Other areas allowed modified veterinary care, typically emergency only, but by reducing the ability of veterinarians to provide preventive care, many of those emergencies were from conditions that were preventable or treatable if caught early but became very serious after the disease or condition took hold. Those pets who were lucky enough to obtain veterinary care were typically much sicker and often had worse outcomes than before the pandemic, when veterinary care had been more readily available. This caused intense stress to the veterinary team.

Additionally, the COVID pandemic stressed almost everyone among the practice's client base. Just living through the pandemic often caused a constant state of uncertainty and stress, and animal owners who confronted closed veterinary clinics and a dramatic decrease in veterinary availability for the animals they loved or worked with were understandably frustrated and unhappy on top of the general stress.

In some cases, this led to angry clients who unfortunately took out their frustration inappropriately on the essential workers, including veterinary doctors and staff. As a result, many veterinary workers left the profession, either temporarily or permanently, causing intense shortages and even more overwork issues for those who remained. It was obvious to me that this veterinary emergency clinic was suffering severely from this type of issue, as clients who were already upset with an animal in distress were faced with long waits for veterinary care and lashed out at the very staff who were still there to treat their pets.

THE BRINK OF COLLAPSE

The day I first arrived back at the emergency clinic, a year after the start of the pandemic, and read the messages from the two remaining managers that they had both left on vacation, I could tell they had been stretched almost beyond bearing. I understood their need to get away; however, I didn't even have keys to the building! They appeared to assume I would step back in after three and a half years away and simply pick up where I had left off.

I quickly realized that the business I had returned to was nothing like the one I had left behind, despite the same name and location. My first S.O.A.P. analysis was, therefore, very simple: Find out what was currently happening.

Once I found a key to get into my old office, I began by meeting with every employee I could convince to come talk to me. At first, the veteran employees who knew me from before were the only ones who accepted my offer to talk, but then others began to make their way in to see me. The talks were very similar, no matter who spoke with me, consisting of a series of complaints and venting. Some of this was the COVID stress that I couldn't fix, but other areas were issues for me to add to my S.O.A.P. analysis. I took copious notes but could easily detect patterns and see what had happened to bring this wonderful business so close to failure.

And I realized quickly that failure was very close. We had less than half of the doctors and staff needed to function appropriately, which meant little revenue. Wages in other local businesses had shot up due to the pandemic, but none of these employees had received raises. The local coffee shop was offering unskilled labor wages that were at or above those of my highly trained veterinary staff! Despite the low wages, many of the staff had remained because they truly loved the mission of caring for pets in need, but they were almost completely burned out and were sadly planning to leave.

So, while I could see a lot of objective issues to address in the wages, revenue, and general operations, I could tell that the true critical need was to address the subjective aspects of the negativity and demoralized staff. My analysis, therefore, started with keeping our people as the number one priority.

Having identified the need to focus on people, I realized that my weeks of speaking with team members had been very helpful. Not only did I get the information I needed, but they also felt heard, and that gave them hope. But I had to work quickly, or I'd lose them to their depression and hopelessness again.

I started a monthly email summary to share updates with the team and counter the lack of transparency many had complained about. This was also a vehicle where I could share inspiring updates and manage the flow of information to decrease damaging rumors and gossip.

Initial Steps Following My S.O.A.P. Notes

My notes from the individual discussions had identified some common pain points, so I started there. It was easy for the staff to blame their supervisors for the problems. I realized that those unfortunate supervisors had been thrust into a difficult situation beyond their training and expertise but had tried the best they could. However, there were obvious improvements that could be made.

For example, I immediately required the middle managers to come to me to discuss any decisions or issues prior to acting on them and to have me present any time they planned to conduct employee performance conversations. I disliked micromanaging, but I needed to identify where their management training and skills were lacking, and I could see no other way to do this.

We instituted a weekly administrative meeting where these young leaders would share information as a group, getting training and advice as best I could give them. I also leaned on a human relations professional consultant to review our policies and performance management plans. Luckily, the managers were truly dedicated and willing to learn, and everyone made great strides.

Although I could see the supervisor team improving, the rest of the staff needed to see more tangible evidence of change. The month after I arrived, my analysis of wages showed me that we had absolutely no chance of keeping our patient care staff unless we dramatically increased employee compensation to meet the prevailing post-pandemic wages, which were about 25 percent higher than before the pandemic for trained veterinary staff. The board of directors balked, and with good reason, as our current revenue did not support this huge wage increase. However, I was adamant that this was the only way to keep our business open. With strong support from the practice consultant the board had hired to lure me back, I made the dramatic wage increase.

The month following the wage increase was nerve-racking. I had committed to this new expense, and our current revenue just barely covered payroll. That would not be sustainable for long, but luckily, we saw immediate improvements. The month after I instituted the large wage increase, our revenue jumped, and then it continued to climb, fully covering the pay increases. Our staff really believed in the mission and wanted to work; they just needed to feel appreciated. In return, they worked hard. The business took off financially and continued to grow.

We still had issues with the subjective side of the business. There was a lot of emotional damage done by the long demoralization, the pandemic, and other issues in veterinary medicine, which has a high mental stress component. I searched for employee resources, such as an Employee Assistance Program that could provide mental health counseling and other support to ease the stress felt by our staff and doctors. I was pleased to get the reports that this program was subsequently used by close to a quarter of our employees. While the benefit was anonymous, so I couldn't know who was using the program or for what service, I was happy to know that at least some of our team found this employee support service to be beneficial.

ORDER RESTORED

My S.O.A.P. analysis needed to be updated frequently as I moved from subjective concerns like staff engagement to objective issues like revenue production and expense management. I likened this dangerous stage of the business to a critical patient in the emergency room, whose condition was changing constantly and needed close monitoring and attention. The business would respond to one area of concern with improvement, but then another would become an issue. It was draining and required a lot of attention from me. As just one person, it was easy to assess that I needed help, so one of my next plans was to create and train a management team.

I was lucky to have a couple of good employees already in management positions, and I identified some others with potential. In my interviews, one department had bemoaned the loss of a well-respected employee I remembered as having management potential. I recruited her back to be the supervisor of that department, and to my delight, she was willing to return and joined my fledgling management team. I then trained and developed these young leaders. It was a difficult situation, with many employees still bitter and jaded, and I tried to shield the management team from the worst of the negativity while gradually increasing their areas of responsibility.

I could now leverage my S.O.A.P. by creating different areas of the business to review, with plans that I could delegate to the management team. Over time, they began to gain confidence and experience, coming up with their own ideas and plans and eventually taking over some distinct areas of responsibility.

As an owner or executive, it is important to realize that teamwork is critical. While that is obvious in large businesses, I have often seen small businesses where the sole owner or key manager thinks they need to handle everything by themselves. This works for a while, but at some point, the owner begins to feel trapped or may experience burnout. An important aspect of any leadership position is creating a team for backup and support. Without a team, the business growth becomes limited by the constraints of the individual manager, but with a team mentality, the business can expand and grow.

Luckily, the veterinary hospital benefited from the management team and the changes that were instituted. The business returned to flourishing, to the point that a large and well-respected national veterinary corporation offered to purchase the now smoothly running veterinary hospital. The board of directors accepted the offer, and I was thrilled to know that our hardworking employees would now have the expanded benefits and opportunities found by being part of a large corporation.

The teamwork had brought our veterinary emergency hospital back from the brink of collapse, returned it to being able to fulfill its mission, and set it on its way to expand with the collaboration of a veterinary group known to be one of the very top in the field.

TAKEAWAYS

- **Management matters to both culture and success**. Attentive managers can identify potential issues before they flare up into real problems and may be able to fix problems in the moment.

- Culture is a subjective aspect of business because it is about the people. Whether a business sells products or services, it still runs by the labor of its people. **A good culture means happy employees** who are more likely to provide good service or products and leave customers happy—a recipe for business success.

- **Sharing information** creates a sense of transparency, which builds trust and helps to create a common culture.

- It is important to create a **team mentality in your business** as it grows. With a team, your business will benefit from additional strengths and creativity beyond a single founder, allowing for expanded business growth and development.

PART III

PRACTICAL APPLICATION
OF S.O.A.P. IN BUSINESS

7

S.O.A.P. FOR YOUR SMALL BUSINESS

I love the concept of a small business. Small businesses are typically started by an individual or a small group with a deep sense of mission. They have an idea, a service, or a product that they know will make a difference for someone else, so they start a new business, hoping their work will have a positive effect and their business will run smoothly so they can make a good living.

Unfortunately, a great idea, helpful service, or exciting product doesn't by itself make a business run, so the owners find themselves pulled away from the mission they love in order to run the business. Paradoxically, to get their beloved idea into the world, they have to decrease the amount of time they spend working on their mission to tend to the business aspects. In some cases, this can crush the joy and excitement that got them started with their business in the first place. It can even result in business failure.

The US Bureau for Labor Statistics 2024 data for small businesses indicates that more than 20 percent fail in the first *year* of business! And only 50 percent are still in business five years after starting.[1] I see this as a terrible waste of potential, which is why I offer the problem-oriented S.O.A.P. system to help support these business owners and keep their dreams alive.

The administrative aspects of running a business commonly sap the energy of these dedicated entrepreneurs. This is a mutual complaint among small-business owners, who now have to spend time learning about "the business of business," no matter what field they are in. Even if the business is successful enough that a practice manager can be hired, it is still very important for the owner to understand enough business to ensure the practice manager is honest and efficient and that the business is running as best it can. The S.O.A.P. system can help identify and organize issues for the business owners (and their practice managers) to work on the most important business aspects in an efficient manner, leaving more time for them to do what they love.

I turned to S.O.A.P. when I was asked to review the workings of a small business with one owner and two locations, and these methodical notes helped organize my thoughts so I could handle a wide variety of issues. Even if a business is small, it is

---

1. "What Percentage of Small Businesses Fail? 2024 Data Reveals the Answer," *Commerce Institute*, https://www.commerceinstitute.com/business-failure-rate/.

still complex. A small business has many of the same aspects as a large corporation: There are clients or customers, employees, facilities, inventory, legal and tax issues, and so on. The only difference is the scale of the operations. I found that the S.O.A.P. method refined the complexity into simpler categories, which helped make important actionable steps more obvious.

In my first management position where I came up with the candy bar reward, the S.O.A.P. review identified a common denominator of staff motivation for the different problems of poor appointment scheduling, increased overtime expense (when staff stayed late to finish clients scheduled at the very end of the day), and decreased overall revenue. The candy bar incentive was a simple motivator that rewarded staff for scheduling more appointments during normal working hours, therefore increasing daily revenue.

Clarifying the normal scheduling hours helped staff understand the importance of appointment timing and, in the process, virtually eliminated the need for overtime staff hours. By identifying the different issues through my S.O.A.P. analysis, I could look at the whole picture and come up with a simple solution to the most pressing issues through the simple staff motivation of a candy bar.

HOW TO APPLY S.O.A.P. ANALYSIS IN YOUR SMALL BUSINESS

Your business is complex and important. To help it run smoothly and effectively, it is worth reviewing and analyzing your whole business from a bird's-eye view. This comprehensive analysis will help you identify issues when you work on your regular S.O.A.P. reviews during the day-to-day running of the business, which will necessarily be smaller in scope. At each step in the analysis, you may find items to add to your strategic to-do list.

Keep track of any items you identify as needing work as you review your business. Writing something on the list doesn't obligate you to fix the issue; recall that you can always keep a to-fix-later section on your problem list if they don't rise to the top in importance as you triage or rank the problem severity. Identifying all potential issues will help you fine-tune your business, increasing your chances of success.

Start by Taking a Step Back

The first step in analyzing your business is to zoom out from the details and look at your business from a larger perspective. Many of us are overwhelmed by all the details of the myriad items on our to-do lists, and it can be very hard to stop fixing everything for this type of exercise. But it will pay dividends to pause the to-do list items for a short time to look at the big picture of your business. Why did you start this business in the first place? What is your mission and your vision for the difference you want to make in the world? Once you have clearly reestablished your "why" for being in business, you can start your analysis.

This starts with identifying the "stakeholders" in your business. These are people for whom your business's success matters.

At the immediate level, this obviously includes the business owner or business partners. If there are investors, who may often be family or friends of the small-business owners, they would also count as stakeholders. Employees have an obvious stake in the success of their employer's business so they can keep their jobs and be paid fairly.

Another obvious stakeholder is the client or customer who wants to purchase the item or service that the business provides. The vendors of products and services your business uses will also want your business to be successful so they can keep you as a customer and get the income for their own businesses from those sales to you.

However, peripheral stakeholders may be less obvious. An example may be the families of the business owners, as the success of the business directly affects them. Families of employees may also be peripheral stakeholders. Another peripheral stakeholder might be the bank that provided a business loan or the landlord that leases out the space for the facility. While these peripheral stakeholders aren't directly tied to the business, issues with these people or entities can have a surprisingly direct impact on the business.

As an example, if the child of a key employee becomes seriously ill, that employee may need to take time off or quit their job. If the landlord decides to sell the building your business operates from, you may find yourself with a dramatic lease increase or even having to move the entire business on short notice.

This exercise in identifying stakeholders is not meant to be frightening; it helps you be realistic in recognizing important factors in your business success and will come in handy later when you are prioritizing items on your S.O.A.P. lists. It will also be a lens from which you can look at business news or local information, such as the possibility of your local bank merging with a large banking corporation, and proactively move on steps to protect your business if one of these stakeholders has a major change that affects your livelihood.

Subjective

Now you will look at the subjective aspects of your business. These are often the hardest to identify because they tend to involve feelings. How do people feel about your business or your product? How do employees feel about their management or business culture? The work you did identifying stakeholders in the previous exercise is very important for this part of reviewing your business. Start with each stakeholder and look at how you can track subjective factors affecting them.

Owner and Partners

The first stakeholder is you, the business owner. I intentionally list this first because many entrepreneurs have become successful by pushing for success at the expense of themselves. Don't skip this step! Look at yourself and identify how you are feeling about your business now. Be honest! Are you still joyful and excited about your business? If yes, are there aspects that you don't like, you ignore, or keep you up at night? Write down how you feel because you, the small-business owner, are the most critical aspect of the entire business.

This will identify if there are any issues under your direct control, so you can address them in your S.O.A.P. plan. Failure to identify issues at this personal level can risk you being blindsided by burnout or depression, especially if you ignore early warning signs by pushing past them until they come crashing down on you.

In a business partner situation, each partner should do this personal analysis on themselves and then each other. If the partners are family or friends, it is also beneficial to look at the underlying family relationship, such as a marriage or the overall friendship. As with the individual, a problem that is ignored ("I don't want to rock the boat" or "It's not that important") tends to build silently and can come up later with very detrimental effects.

Part of this analysis may also involve looking at any documentation of partner agreements. A good agreement should spell out what happens in various situations, including if one partner wants out of the partnership. Having this all spelled out formally and legally can provide significant peace of mind, easing some of the subjective pressure of a partnership. Similarly, any investor agreements should be protected by legal documentation. If you notice any documentation missing that would protect you and your partners and investors, write it on your list so you will remember to correct this oversight.

The Employees

Your employees are a significant factor in your business, whether you employ a single employee or a large team. Without them, you would not be able to provide the full range of services for your clients or get your products made and into the customers' hands in a timely fashion.

You will likely find that many of the subjective issues you deal with in the course of your business are related to having employees. Each employee added means another person with an opinion, a work ethic, a schedule, and a personal life that has to interact with your business and with you, your managers, and other employees. Employees are not parts in a machine that can be swapped out quickly and easily. Depending on the viewpoint of the owners, interacting with employees can be the joy of the business or the most frustrating aspect of each day.

Regardless of whether you are lit up by interacting with your team or not, it is extremely important that your employees like their jobs. While it may have been enough in past economies to simply say, "I pay them, so they should be happy enough," that isn't enough to keep employees happy and engaged anymore. A large segment of the population wants to work a job they believe in, for a product they love and use, or have a career that they feel betters the world in some way. This puts significant subjective pressure on the owners and managers.

How do you determine if your employees like their jobs? You could turn to surveys for employee engagement or employee satisfaction, but those work best in larger organizations with enough staff to ensure survey responses will be confidential. If you only have a few employees, it makes more sense to interact directly with each employee.

For example, if an employee puts in notice to leave, an exit interview would be a useful tool to use. I have received some of the most honest and useful information through exit interviews. Obviously, if they've put in notice, they are relieved of the potential threat of being fired, and the usefulness of feedback you receive during these types of interviews can be surprising.

As an illustration, when I first took over the veterinary emergency clinic, before I had identified the embezzler as the main issue, I had to let an employee go for an unfortunately serious infraction. At her exit interview, she let me know of a lot of operational issues and outright lies told by the hospital director, which helped me identify areas to research. Since he was the immediate supervisor of all the staff, no one who wanted to remain working was willing to speak up about these issues. But by having the exit interview with the departing employee, I learned of issues that otherwise might have remained hidden.

However, there is an inherent issue with the exit interview: They are leaving your employ! The cost to advertise, hire, and train a new employee is significant, so good businesses try to reduce turnover and keep their employees. Consider utilizing "stay interviews," which are conversations with employees designed to listen to them and have them feel recognized and valued. In the process, you can ask for specific feedback, such as how they feel about an operational change, new manager, or other issue, and you can ask what they like about their job and what they think could be improved. If nothing else, simply listen.

When I returned to the emergency facility after being away for almost four years, and found a negative culture on my subjective review, I sat down one-on-one with almost every staff member as part of my initial fact-finding. Although I didn't officially name these as "stay interviews," that is essentially what they were. I met with the employees individually and asked them why they were working here, what they liked about their jobs, and what they needed from management to do their jobs better. In this way, I found the operational problems that were sore spots for the team but not always noticeable to the supervisory team. These were often "minor" issues in the grand scheme, but fixing them made the staff feel heard.

For example, in one set of these early stay interviews, I learned that the staff were frustrated that the clipper blades they used to prepare animals for surgery weren't very sharp, meaning it took longer to shave the surgery site. It was a quick, inexpensive fix to have the clipper blades sent out for sharpening, and the staff were extremely happy with this fix.

By discovering and addressing that issue, I improved the culture because the staff felt valued and heard. This, in turn, gave me credibility as a manager so that the staff were more likely to trust me when I made much larger changes to the business (like when I moved the business from after-hours to a full 24/7/365 emergency clinic). The stay interviews helped me learn about the employees and discover issues I may otherwise not have learned about in a timely manner. This improved the overall culture and trust in the team.

In some cases, social media can be useful in gauging how your employees feel about the business. If you have social media sites, do your employees interact with those sites? Do they proudly let their friends know they work at your business? This is not as direct as simply speaking with your employees, but it still can be a possible method of identifying a potential employee culture issue. Employees who love and feel proud of their employment are likely to stay and generally provide the best customer service.

Customers/Clients

Customers are the next stakeholders to investigate. Happy *and* unhappy customers tell their friends about you, and you want those conversations to be primarily positive. This drives new customers to you through word of mouth and is an excellent source of new business.

How do you find out if your customers are happy? One method is to simply ask them! Many businesses have a system of asking for feedback or sending a survey to customers shortly after they leave the business or finish with the transaction. This can be as simple as a paper form handed out, or it could be questionnaires sent to the customer through text and email communications. While this may be an expense, it has value as it helps identify potential issues right away.

No business is perfect, and every employee has a bad day, so having an upset customer isn't unusual. However, if you can identify that upset customer and interact with them positively right away, there is a good chance you can change their view of your business from negative to positive.

Whether or not you collect customer feedback surveys, it is easy in the internet age to learn how customers feel about your business through a plethora of review sites. However, the very fact that there are so many review sites makes it difficult to keep up. If your business is quite small and local, you may be fine with looking mainly at local review sites, but you may find your business reviewed in places you don't expect. Depending on the size of your business, you may want to have an employee trained to handle your digital interactions or outsource this by hiring a marketing firm. The intent of digital reputation management is to quickly identify digital issues that may show up as bad reviews or negative social media posts and deal with them quickly and effectively to leave a positive digital impression. Even if one angry customer cannot be made happy, a quick and appropriate response will help other potential customers see your business as responsive and concerned.

A related aspect of your marketing to customers is the management of your overall online presence. For most businesses, new customers are likely to search the internet for businesses using various keywords or phrases. You need to make sure those words prompt the internet to show them your business name in response and preferably on the very first page or first few lines of their search. How do you do that? Here is another area where a good marketing team skilled in search engine optimization (SEO) may be a very smart investment.

Finally, another subjective aspect to work on regarding customer stakeholders is your advertising presence. Depending on your specific business, location, and number of competitors, you may need to have an intensive advertising campaign or a very modest one, but some type of marketing is a requirement of most businesses. The type of advertising may change if you are marketing to the public, a specific subset of people, or to other businesses, but this is likely to be a necessary expense for almost every business.

If your business is very small and local and you have good word of mouth, you may be able to avoid significant advertising costs, but you would also be at risk if a more tech-savvy competitor moved in. Whether or not you choose to put money into formal advertising, you will need a sign or an open house or some other way to identify your business to potential customers and clients.

Even if you don't like the thought of marketing or advertising, the fact is that most businesses will not be noticed unless there is some formal way you can announce your presence, point out the value of your service, or identify why your product is one the customer needs or wants, which all fall under the umbrella term of marketing. Analysis of your marketing strategy is an important aspect of your initial S.O.A.P. subjective data analysis.

Objective

For many business owners, finding the objective data is a lot easier than determining the subjective, less concrete aspects of their business. Subjective data is related to amorphous feelings, thoughts, and impressions, while objective data can more easily be measured. What can be measured can more easily be managed, so some business owners may find the objective aspects of this business review to be easier.

The first question here is what data to measure. Some data will be very specific to an individual business, but there are some key overarching categories that all businesses need to handle. The financial aspects of the business are critical, and I find that this is the best place to start. Depending on the size of the business, the owners may handle all the financials by themselves or might involve an employee, a bookkeeper, or an accountant. Financial documents are important for tracking, analysis, and tax purposes at a minimum, so be prepared to review them as well.

A business works by selling a service or a product and receiving payment, so the place to start is to review the system for receiving orders or accepting clients and how they pay the business. If your business uses in-person cash by anyone other than the owner, then you need to ensure appropriate cash controls are in place. This means that a different person receives and tracks the cash, another verifies cash counts and creates the bank deposits, and a third reconciles the bank statement. While this can be problematic in very small businesses, failure to utilize this three-person minimum opens up the business to the risk of having cash disappear inappropriately, through embezzlement or theft, as I found while analyzing the financials of the emergency clinic.

If your business is paid by credit card, it is wise to review the finance charge your bank assesses your business. This is the percentage of the money received that is collected by the bank for the convenience of processing a credit card, and fees can creep up unnoticed by many business owners. Other bank fees can also be reviewed at the same time. Banks want your business, and your banking needs can change over time, so it may be wise at intervals to compare banks to determine if your current bank is the best for your business now.

If you utilize an online store or sell your product through a large online distributor, it is wise to review the terms and functions of the system at intervals. Order something from your own store now and then to make sure the order process still works correctly. It is surprising how many businesses do not check their basic business process like this. Something as simple as a faulty computer update could break the links to your order page, and you could lose a lot of business without knowing it unless you have some method of checking your system regularly.

Whether you see clients for a service or sell products to a customer or another business, it is important to track your sales numbers. If the numbers drop, identify the reason immediately, mitigating it promptly if possible. Communication with the customer or customer-facing employees will be very important if the reason is out of your control or likely to last a long time. For instance, if a product is on back order, promptly notifying the affected customer is better than waiting until they angrily contact your business after they fail to receive the item at the expected time.

Ensure the business has a method of tracking all income received and expenses incurred. There are simple software packages for small businesses to use, or a bookkeeper or an accountant can be hired to do the work of creating appropriate documentation and recording all transactions. Reviewing your financial documents, such as the balance sheet and the profit-and-loss statement, will identify where most of your expenses come from. In service industries, labor and payroll are likely the highest expense. In product sales, the cost of production or cost of goods sold should be carefully tracked.

If your business is in an industry that has published KPIs,

count yourself lucky and use them to compare your business's performance. Is the KPI for labor costs for your type of business 35 percent? How does that compare with your actual labor costs? While your business is unlikely to track the exact numbers of the published KPIs, you should be fairly close. If an area of your expenses is dramatically higher than the KPI, a deeper investigation into that aspect is warranted.

If you don't have published KPIs and you are not a start-up business, then a comparison of your numbers to the previous year is helpful. Was your inventory on hand 15 percent of the business last year and 20 percent this year? Maybe your purchaser is ordering too much at a time and a review of the purchasing parameters is warranted. I like to compare using percentages rather than dollars since businesses may have a growth or slowdown of sales, which skews the dollar amounts, but the percentages should remain similar and can be better used for comparisons.

Assessment

As you reviewed your business from the perspective of this big-picture-style S.O.A.P. analysis, you probably added items that were potential or known problems to a list. Now is the time for an analysis of that problem list. Look for patterns or items that might go together. For instance, if you notice that your employees often complain about their supervisor and you also see that you've had a lot of employee turnover, those two items might be related. A bad manager often drives staff away. If your customer reviews complain about their phone interactions, and your receptionist is going through a divorce and often in a bad mood, those two problems could be related.

Even if the patterns aren't obvious, group the problems into similar categories. For example, you may see that you have a lot of little issues and problems with computers, phones, technology, and so on. When you group them together, you may realize that these all fall under the category of Information Technology, and the simple solution to all of these may be to work with an IT support firm or hire your brilliant "techie" niece to help! By combining similar issues like this, your action list for potential solutions will get shorter.

During this phase, don't forget about those issues that include yourself! You started your business with a lot of great ideas for your product or service, but there is a good chance that those ideas did not include all the various aspects of business. This is the time to be brutally honest with yourself. If you note a lot of employee problems, and you are essentially the main manager, the solution may be for you to look into management skills training for yourself. If calculating payroll each pay period eats up your family time, it may be worth looking into a payroll service to take that off your plate. If your inventory costs are high, or you are plagued by running out of key items just when you need them, a course in inventory management is likely to pay for itself quickly and be worth the investment.

When the problems include you, look into either improving your knowledge or delegating the issue to someone else. Avoid the common entrepreneurial trap of thinking you must do everything yourself. Yes, you may be able to perform the task faster, better, or more accurately, but in many cases, delegating to someone else will leave you more time and peace of mind. With that freed-up time, you can now work on the business aspects you do well and love. The owner is often the main revenue producer in a small business, so the more time you can spend growing your business and producing revenue, the easier it will be to pay for that employee or vendor who is now performing the other task you dislike, and the happier you will be!

Prioritize the List of Problems

Now that you have identified and consolidated problems, you will need to order the items on your list according to what you think is most important. It is probable that there will be too many issues to tackle at once, so you have to prioritize. Sometimes, the order is obvious. If not, there are a variety of prioritization systems available.

A very simple tool I use for quick sorting of a list is to look at each item from two perspectives: 1) the importance to the overall mission of the business and 2) how quickly it must be done. This is a variation of the more important/less important and more urgent/less urgent matrix system that is also commonly used. My quick-sort method assigns a number 1, 2, or 3 to each item regarding how important it is to the business's mission and then a similar 1, 2, or 3 number to indicate how quickly this must be handled. Each item will have two numbers, and I add them up. The lowest number possible will be 2 (1 + 1), and the highest possible will be 6 (3 + 3). I then rework the list based on these numbers, with the lowest number first on my list.

Quick-Sort Example

UNSORTED PROBLEMS PRIORITIZATION

Problems identified from S.O.A.P. analysis	Importance to mission	Timeliness	Total
Multiple IT problems group	2	3	5
High employee turnover	1	2	3
Family stress from owner doing payroll	2	2	4
Constantly missing key inventory items	1	1	2

Table 7.1: Unsorted Problems Prioritization

When deciding on the numbers, you get to choose your parameters. For instance, if your list to be sorted is items to do that day, your timeliness number scheme might be 1 for "do in the morning," 2 for "do in the afternoon," and 3 for "do if you have time."

On the other hand, if you are working on problems for the year, you might have your 1 for "focus on this quarter," 2 for "next quarter," and 3 for "end of year." Likewise, you are the business owner, so you get to decide how important an item is to the mission of your business. This is *your* prioritization list.

In Table 7.1, looking at the numbers in the "Total" column will provide the order in which you tackle the list.

PROBLEMS PRIORITIZED

Reordered problems identified from S.O.A.P. analysis	Total
Constantly missing key inventory items	2
High employee turnover	3
Family stress from owner doing payroll	4
Multiple IT problems group	5

Table 7.2: Problems Prioritized

With your list clearly prioritized, you are now ready to make your plan of action.

Plan

Now that you have identified and prioritized the problems, you can get to work on making a difference right away. In Table 7.2, you would see that fixing the inventory issues is the first area of focus. You identified it as critical to your business (1 for "Mission") since missing inventory means you can't fill orders or serve clients, and that is an immediate risk to your financial health and reputation. You also identified this as an issue to deal with right away (1 for "Timeliness"). While the other items were important enough for you to put them on the list and should be dealt with, you should wait until you have started steps toward the solution of your top problem.

A danger here is getting stuck in the planning stage, spending time looking at each item, and writing careful steps for each. Instead, treat this like an emergency doctor would treat a critical patient; deal with the critical (top) problems first, then move to the next problems on the list. Sometimes, you may even find that when you fully handle the higher-priority items, the lower-priority items drop off the list as either fixed or no longer important. Spending time at the outset making plans for these lower-level problems keeps you from addressing the critical issues in a timely fashion. I recommend working on your problems from the top of the prioritized list to the bottom.

Of course, you often don't have the luxury of working only on one problem at a time, but by prioritizing, you can start to take steps toward fixing the most important problem and then move to the next problem. Large issues like this often need multistep solutions, which can take time.

Let's look at the assessment example in Table 7.2, Problems Prioritized. You have identified a problem with inventory. Perhaps your immediate action step would be to walk through your storage area to review the organization and identify any missing items. You might also register for an inventory management course you found through an online webinar that will be running next week to improve your knowledge of the subject.

Say you have a little time left today, so you move to the next problem on your list, which is the high employee turnover. You decide on a plan to start stay interviews with your current employees so they feel heard and can help you identify the source of the problem. Your next step will be to schedule those, but you decide that you can wait until tomorrow for that step. You leave for the day already having made significant progress toward addressing the top two of the four problems.

Your action steps for the next day are also clear, as you will be addressing any inventory shortages you found today and starting to schedule the staff stay interviews. After those steps, you will start researching payroll support vendors and possibly scheduling meetings with them over the next week. Next week, you will have the staff interviews and attend the inventory management webinar along with meeting those vendors.

As you handle those issues, you realize that you are well on your way to resolving your three worst problems. As time allows, you begin to research IT solutions (maybe calling that niece of yours in for a job interview!). By focusing your attention on the prioritized problem list and following through with steps based on that priority, you will be amazed at how quickly and efficiently you can clean up your business issues with the S.O.A.P. method!

TAKEAWAYS

- Start with **a bird's-eye view** to see the big picture of your business. This will include clarifying your mission and vision—the "why" of your business—and making sure that this hasn't gotten lost in the day-to-day grind of keeping the business functioning.

- Identify your stakeholders. **Stakeholders are the people who have a vested interest in your business being successful.** This includes obvious stakeholders such as owners and customers but also the less obvious ones such as employees, vendors, and even family members in some cases.

- Next, review the **subjective aspects**, including the workplace culture, customer satisfaction, social media, and marketing presence.

- Now review the **objective factors**, such as the financial documents (profit and loss, balance sheet), trends in sales and customer base, and other typical business data. If you are lucky enough to be in an industry with KPIs for your type of business, use these to compare your data with ideals and identify issues to work on for improvement.

- The **assessment phase** is where you put the puzzle pieces of your business issues into similar categories, looking for patterns or underlying common factors. Without this step, the list of problems to fix simply becomes an overwhelming to-do list. By organizing them into categories, you can more easily identify action steps that will make a difference and improve your business.

- With all the work you've done already, you may find the **plan starts to form itself** naturally. By organizing similar issues and identifying common denominators, you will see actions that will correct the issues.

- **Organize your action steps** to address the biggest, most severe issues first. In this way, you start with some big wins and then can buy time to address the other issues that may not be as serious. This follows the idea of medical triage, where you work on the most severe issues to the overall business.

8

S.O.A.P. FOR THE LARGE BUSINESS ENTITY

Managing a large business entity dramatically increases the number of issues you need to handle. As the business grows, so does the management team and the need for delegation. When I took on a position managing multiple hospitals and projects in a university setting, my first comment to myself was, "I need to up my delegation game!" A large business requires a large team, and this adds the dimension of team and project management to the task management focus more common in a smaller business.

Here, the problem-oriented S.O.A.P. method can be extremely helpful because you can scale it to fit your needs. You can use the S.O.A.P. format to review your overall strategic plan and big-picture goals, but you can also use it to support your team as you organize and delegate projects and tasks to them. The S.O.A.P. method can be used to help you and your team keep track of a huge job with many aspects in an organized and clear fashion.

For a large business entity, it is extremely helpful to start with the strategic plan. The first step for a strategic plan is to look honestly at where you are now. You can't make a plan to get to a goal if you don't know your starting point! Therefore, my first recommendation is to get a clear idea of what's happening in the business right now. This can sometimes be uncomfortable because it includes identifying all the pain points, but it is a crucial step. The S.O.A.P. method can help you review all aspects of the business for a complete analysis, supporting a very effective strategic plan.

STRATEGIC PLAN S.O.A.P.

It is surprising that many businesses do not create an effective strategic plan. I suspect it is a leadership training issue. Many business managers come up through the ranks, being promoted because they are good at various operational aspects in their particular field, but they often have limited training in strategic thinking. Their decision-making is necessarily tactical and operational, and that becomes their comfort zone.

As managers rise up in ranks toward an executive level,

they must first learn to delegate and support their teams. That is sometimes difficult for anyone who has created their success as a powerful individual contributor, and it takes time. When they master that process, they may rise to the next level as an executive leader. Suddenly, they are asked to think and act strategically, which is probably quite different from the thinking processes they previously used along their leadership success path. Unsurprisingly, the strategic plans they create may be very tactical and operational rather than truly strategic.

For example, imagine a business has an issue with tardiness. At the supervisory level, the manager might focus attendance issues on the actions of individual contributors and work on performance management of each individual's schedule and work hours. At the strategic level, the executive might look for an underlying cause, such as employees coming in late because their shift starts when the area's rush hour is busiest. At the operational level, the manager will be stuck working to change each individual's behavior, while the strategic executive might propose altering shift start and end times to be before or after the rush hour. The S.O.A.P. method is a useful tool to start with operational data to inform a strategic thought process.

First, here are some definitions. *Strategy* is "a plan, method, or series of maneuvers or stratagems for obtaining a specific goal or result."[1] *Strategic thinking* is the art of creating that plan to meet

---

1. "Strategy," Dictionary.com, https://www.dictionary.com/browse/strategy/.

the goal. *Tactics* are the "specific steps that are taken to actualize goals in the short term and long term in an organization. Tactics are influenced by an organization's strategic goals."[2]

Note that tactics are the operational steps many managers are already utilizing, but they are (or should be) informed by the overall strategy. For example, if your business makes swimsuits, your strategic plan would encompass water sports and clothing, but you would not need to include winter sports ideas in your goals. Then, your tactical steps would support the water sports or clothing areas and skip any steps pertinent to winter sports.

When I was overseeing the several different hospitals at the veterinary college, they were all slightly different, based on the population of animals they served. Four of the hospitals supported large animals but in different ways. There was an ambulatory service for horse owners, where veterinary professionals would drive out to treat horses in their home pastures and barns. This hospital was focused on treatments that could be performed in a "field" setting for horses that were either companions or performance animals (like a racehorse).

There was also a formal hospital for horses at the veterinary school. This was for horses with issues that couldn't be handled on a farm, such as a major surgery or a serious illness. The medications and instruments needed by each of these two units were different,

---

2. "What Are Business Tactics?," Professional Leadership Institute, https://professional leadershipinstitute.com/resources/what-are-business-tactics/.

despite both treating horses. Additionally, the training and exper-tise of the doctors and staff were different for each unit, including specialty services. There was a similar pair of units that treated large animals associated with agriculture, such as cattle, swine, poultry, etc. Because of agricultural constraints regarding the food supply, these units had different medications and procedures from the equine units, even though they all treated large animals.

On the small-animal side, the teaching hospital offered not only general veterinary care, but also a series of specialty ser-vices, each with different equipment, medications, and staffing needs. Finally, there were units that provided emergency services, including a free-standing pet emergency hospital in a nearby urban center. The operational and tactical needs of each hospital differed because of the population of animals they served, even though all fell under the overarching strategic mission of the vet-erinary college.

When reviewing your business to identify the current sit-uation, it is helpful to review big-picture ideas, like marketing or supply and demand. There will be time later to dig deep into details, but start with where you are now as a general trend or idea. However, it is still useful to use the S.O.A.P. divisions in this review.

As described in the previous chapter for small businesses, it is extremely important to identify your stakeholders. These might include customers and clients, employees, shareholders and own-ers, and vendors. There may also be peripheral stakeholders, such as employees' families, the industry or profession you are in, the government, and even the general public, depending on the size and scope of your business. These are people or entities for whom the success of your business matters at some level.

Subjective

Using the S.O.A.P. format, you would start your big-picture review with the subjective aspects. What do people think about your company, your products, or your services? Review this from the standpoint of each of the stakeholders. If there are owners, a board of directors, or shareholders, start there. What is their stated goal for the business? It is obvious that keeping the business alive and functioning is a key goal, but there is also undoubtedly a mission and a vision for the enterprise. This should be the lens through which you analyze your strategic plan. Is the stated mission and vision a match for the demands of the ownership stakeholders? If not, this would be the first area of concern to identify for your analysis.

Next, look at who your business serves. If the business manufactures items, what do your customers think of the products? If you run a service business, what is the viewpoint of the clients? In the digital age, this information can readily be found online. Although you can start with customer satisfaction surveys (You *do* have them, right? Or is that the next item on your list of issues to address?), don't stop there. The internet can be scary and direct and will likely show you the dark underbelly of what some people think of your business.

As painful as it may be, read those review rants or angry blogs about your company. Look to see if there are common themes. Do several of the bad reviews mention rude customer service personnel? Add that problem to your list. Is there a frequent complaint about delays in promised product delivery? Another problem to list. Of course, there will always be random irrational complaints, and I am not suggesting that you list each of those, but search for any trends that may indicate an area of concern for you to address.

Since subjective data can be difficult to quantify, you may need to use multiple sources and then extrapolate the data across these sources to get an idea of some of the views of your business. You could use online reviews or survey data of customers, conduct formal or informal surveys of employees, and read published materials from the company, then investigate the commentary or discussions of those materials. It is important to review all the data, both good and bad. We are all human, and we tend to prefer positive and complimentary information. However, failing to learn what the detractors are saying leaves you open to being blindsided in the competitive world of business.

Take a deep breath and then find out what your direct competitors say about your business. It is surprising how much you can discover with this simple strategy. Does your competitor advertise better customer service than "the others" (implying your business)? Maybe they have heard issues about the customer service in your business and are trying to use that to their advantage. Write down all that you discover, even if it is contradictory. The larger the data set you investigate, the more likely you will get various opposite viewpoints. However, you can still tease out important trends, pain points, or areas of strength from this type of review. These should all be captured on your list of issues found in the subjective sphere.

Your employees are another major stakeholder group. The information from Chapter 7 on how to identify what your employees think is just as pertinent for a large operation as a small business, so I will not repeat it here. The only additional factor for a larger enterprise is that you may have a very different employee culture and experience in different units or divisions, so make sure to evaluate each unit separately. You will also have the addition of a management team. It is also very important to include the thoughts of your leaders in the subjective section of your analysis.

Objective

With a large business, you would typically have a fairly robust set of objective data. Each department or unit will likely have created reports over a significant amount of time that you can review. This is an advantage as you create your initial strategic review. However, it is important to maintain a healthy skepticism. Department heads or unit directors will generally have created fairly glowing reports to highlight accomplishments and minimize problems in their sector of control. It is extremely important to review the data to look for areas of concern.

A good review of the objective data will include comparing these reports over time for the individual unit or department and then comparing across the units. When reviewing over time, ensure the reports include similar data.

In one case I was involved in, an academic institution changed the parameters of their financial data year over year. One year, payroll figures included only staff wages, while management salaries were rolled into administrative costs, and teacher salaries were included in academic costs. The following year, the payroll financial report included staff and administration salaries together, with a separate item for administration and academic costs, without identifying faculty salaries. The third year combined all payroll into one amount. It was impossible to tease out a change year over year. While this could have been innocent, this type of change can also be used to escape careful scrutiny. In fact, this institution folded within a few years due to lack of financial oversight.

To compare across units, I find that focusing on percentages rather than absolute numbers helps even out the data. Most profit and loss reports can be configured to show real numbers and percentages, so I look at both to get a more robust picture of each department. While one unit may have sales of $500,000 and another \$10.5M, similar units should still have similar percentages for sales, expenses, employee numbers, and so on. If one business unit has 20 percent costs of goods sold (COGS) and the other runs at 10 percent COGS for a similar enterprise, it is worth noting. Capture the positives and the negatives because your strategic plan will need both to be effective.

Assessment

Now comes the fun part of synthesizing the overview data you have reviewed and finding trends, strengths, and weaknesses. To organize the large problem list you have likely created, I like spreadsheets, where I can arrange lists in rows with different columns of pertinent data I can sort from.

As an example, if I noted a high employee turnover in one department, I would list the problem but also include a column for the specific department, the manager, and maybe the type of work being performed. After listing all the problems with this level of detail, I can sort the spreadsheet by any of those columns. That way, I could compare the number of problems by department, sort issues by manager, or evaluate problems in specific areas of the labor force across all departments. This helps me identify trends at a macro level that may otherwise be obscured.

While the list of problems you have found may individually look daunting, when you evaluate them and find overall trends, you minimize the complexity and increase your opportunity to make meaningful changes. In the previous example, if you have many different employee issues, but upon sorting, you realize these are all found in areas managed by one supervisor, your action step is obvious. By training or replacing that one supervisor, you will make headway in improving all the problems you had individually listed that were under the purview of that supervisor. This is the advantage of collecting your data at the micro level but then sorting and analyzing for big trends.

Plan Preparation

Once you have identified these macro issues, it is time to make an overall action plan. Even after sorting these into larger trends and issues, you may still be presented with a large number of issues to address. This can be overwhelming as you try to evaluate what to do in a realistic timeframe. Here is where we circle back to the strategic plan. Your strategic plan will be the context from which you operate to determine the importance of dealing with each of the trends and the order in which you will address those issues.

The SWOT Analysis: Strengths, Weaknesses, Opportunities, Threats

While there are many different methods for working out an effective strategic plan, I find that a SWOT (Strengths, Weaknesses, Opportunities, Threats) analysis is simple and fairly quick. You can always flesh out the sections into a detailed narrative if you need to create a report for a board of directors or a higher-level executive. You should create a SWOT for the entire enterprise to guide your overall plan. You can also create subsidiary SWOT analyses for individual units or departments if the business is large enough to warrant that level of detailed strategy, but those should follow the enterprise SWOT.

The strengths would list what your company does well, either as a whole or in a specific unit. These would be items you might want to build on eventually, but certainly preserve and protect them for now. You may find that items could be placed in more than one category. For instance, if your tried-and-true product is well known and beloved by consumers, that would be a strength. If there is a competitor creating a very good copy of that product, that would be a threat. If there were a supply chain issue that regularly slows the production of that item, that would be a weakness.

The weaknesses would be areas you have identified that hinder the accomplishment of your mission or vision. Here is where you would analyze your data in context. To return to my previous example of a company that made water sports clothing, having a shortage of winter clothing material would not be a true weakness on a SWOT, because the mission and vision of that company did not include having a winter clothing line. However, a shortage of material used to make the water sports clothing would directly affect the stated mission and would be listed as a weakness.

The opportunities section is where you can let your creativity fly. This involves a vision of future possibilities. Have you noticed the weakness of a competitor that could be exploited by an aggressive ad campaign? That would be a potential opportunity. Do you see a market demand for an ancillary product that is in the scope of your mission and vision? Creating a unit to make that product may be an opportunity. Does your service industry have a growth opportunity in a neighboring city? That could be an opportunity as well.

I like using this section to move the business forward. This is where you float the big ideas that could really grow your enterprise. It doesn't mean the idea will move forward, but it can help expand what is possible for the business in meaningful ways that help drive future plans.

The threats section can be difficult to write. Many executives have risen up the ranks by getting results and focusing on those accomplishments, often minimizing problems unless they have been overcome. They may be very focused on the present or immediate past in their business reports. However, it is impossible to be completely successful without anticipating and identifying potential future threats to the business. It can be uncomfortable because it involves a worst-case scenario type of thinking, which may be difficult for executives who thrive on being inspiring and uplifting. Identifying possible problems can feel pessimistic and defeatist, but it is not. Brainstorming about what could go wrong helps you set up a prevention plan that will keep your business strong.

Your analysis of trends and a review of weaknesses may help you see possible threats. If you have high employee turnover, for instance, look at what could happen if that worsened rather than improved. If inflation costs steadily rise, consider what an economic downturn would do to your business. Even your strengths should be analyzed for possible threats. For example, if your business's strength rides on the production or actions of a star employee, what would happen if that employee left the business? The point of this section is to identify danger areas so you can work on mitigating the effects should one of those threats come to pass.

You have now captured a clear snapshot of your business, both the good and the bad, and identified important areas to work on that fit the mission and vision of your business. The time spent on this analysis has created a very valuable road map for you. Now is the time to move these ideas forward with an action plan!

Your Working Action Plan

The action plan is how you create the structure to keep your business on track and constantly improve. Depending on the size of the business or your area of control, you can create one action plan or break it into smaller chunks for delegation to others. This is where you refer back to the list of problems you created and organize by department, manager, or other unit of action. Then, triage the list from problems or actions of highest importance to those of least importance to your mission and goals.

If you use a spreadsheet to capture all the problems, it is then easy to sort the problems by unit or manager. Alternatively, you can create a simple list for each manager. Now separate each subunit and prioritize the problems, combining similar problems where possible (such as the example of multiple employee issues all resulting from one manager). Depending on the structure of your business and the strength of your management team, develop a plan for resolving the most important problems either by yourself or in brainstorming sessions with those leaders. This should be tailored to each unit, and you will need to be sure the management team is on board with these actions. Ensure that your action plan includes a timeline.

As the leader of a large enterprise, your next step may be the hardest because you need to step back and let your team manage the action steps. Typical top executives are high achievers and are used to driving results. However, it is important to let your managers manage their areas of control. Not only do you create strong leaders but you also avoid the stress and burnout you would feel if you tried to handle all the action steps yourself. Your job now becomes one of managing the managers. You will need to inspire the team and provide support. You also should have a system to check back in with the managers to have them report on their progress or any issues. This is the art of delegation, and it is a very important skill for you to develop and use.

Overseeing a large business entity can seem like a vast and overwhelming task, but the problem-oriented S.O.A.P. structure can help simplify management into effective and efficient steps that make a huge difference with minimal effort. The time you spend analyzing the business and reviewing it from a big-picture perspective, coupled with your mission and vision, can easily move your business to increasing success. The S.O.A.P. system can bring back the fun and excitement of running even a very large enterprise, keeping alive the mission to make that one special difference in the world that drove the original formation of the business.

TAKEAWAYS

- For a large entity, a **formal strategic plan** is necessary to identify the overall context based on the mission and vision of the organization.

- **Strategic thinking is separate from tactical and operational thinking**, and it is a skill that may need to be honed in executives who have risen up the ranks from an operational position. The strategic plan will inform the later tactical operations.

- **Strategic action plans in a large organization** may take the form of a SWOT analysis, identifying strengths, weaknesses, opportunities, and threats. The S.O.A.P. analysis can inform the executive leadership on issues that can be organized into the common SWOT format and presented to guide leaders.

- The **strategic action plan can be broken down into sections** pertinent for different units or departments in the larger business entity, and then local leadership can use their individual S.O.A.P. analysis to identify tactical and operational action steps for their areas of responsibility to improve the business while following the overall strategy developed by higher leadership.

- Utilize **delegation and people-leader management** to extend your action reach in a large organization.

CONCLUSION

───

YOUR BUSINESS IS BUILT TO MAKE A DIFFERENCE

Your business was created to make a difference in the world, whether through producing something tangible, creating ideas, or serving others. Your business matters, and you know that because people are willing to pay for what you do there. Whether you are an entrepreneur, a small-business owner, a middle manager, or an executive at a large corporation, you and your business are driven by a purpose—an intrinsic mission.

While this mission drives the formation and continued action of your business, it is essential that the business be successful in order to continue making the difference it was designed for. Whether you are a seasoned executive, a manager who has risen up the ranks, or an entrepreneur driven by a singular passion, the simple S.O.A.P. technique can help you analyze and effectively act to improve your business and meet the mission that drives your enterprise.

I love businesses with a mission, and I feel proud when the logical thought process of the problem-oriented S.O.A.P. can help keep such a business afloat—just as I saw when correcting the failing satellite clinic I first managed and discovering the financial mismanagement that threatened the emergency hospital. You can use the tools of this method to keep your treasured business fulfilling its mission.

You now can identify the subjective and objective aspects of your business, recognizing trends to see the big picture. You understand the concept of triage and can use that knowledge to prioritize the issues you have identified according to their importance to your overall business mission and goals. You can use your analysis of the problems identified to create a clear and effective action plan, which you can either implement yourself or delegate to others.

I hope this book has helped you simplify the management aspects of leading a business and allowed you to return to the mission that led you to this business in the first place. Thank you for making a difference in the world through the successful management of your business!

ACKNOWLEDGMENTS

This book could not have been written without the many veterinary teams who trusted me to handle the behind-the-scenes details where they work or learn so they could get on with their mission to serve animals in need. Veterinary medicine attracts passionate people who put the health of their patients above their own, time and time again. My life has been touched by so many in the profession. Each of you matters, and I honor you for everything you do for the animals in your care, whether seen or unseen.

Thank you to Marcia for believing in me and for your mentorship! Your trust in my abilities and your constant support over many years allowed me to serve with joy as a veterinarian in your wonderful practice and to value the importance of seeing the "bigger picture" as you encouraged me to join professional boards to give back and make a difference.

Thank you to Joe, who saw and nurtured my leadership in academia, an entirely new area to me, and for trusting your beloved program to me while still being willing to set me free for other opportunities when they arose. You were a calm presence who could still be firm and fight for what was right. You embody servant leadership by taking on all the difficult tasks with no fanfare and easily giving recognition and praise to those around you.

Thank you to Dan for demonstrating caring, personalized leadership. Somehow, you balance myriad disparate views and constant crises while effectively running a large institution, yet you make everyone at any level feel personally special as an individual. You make a complex position appear easy, and you bring much-needed calm when situations try to spiral down. I was lucky to work under your leadership during the difficult years of the COVID pandemic.

Thank you to Jim for unknowingly making a difference to me as an incoming veterinary student through your poise as a final-year veterinary student during my initial new student orientation. Little did I know we would later be colleagues and work together on multiple projects, boards, and entities over the years. You have made a huge difference for the community you serve, and I am honored to have worked in partnership with you in several of those.

Thank you to Jean and Laura for our PVW ("powerful veterinary women") meetings, mixing fun social events with serious business problem-solving discussions. I am so lucky to have friends who are just as obsessed as I am with our profession, have that curious blend of personal and professional interests, and have supportive and understanding partners when we have a PVW triple date!

Lastly, thank you to all the aspiring business owners and managers who have trusted me to help develop their own leadership knowledge and styles. Empowering you as you grow in your leadership meets my own personal mission. You are the future.

INDEX

ABOUT THE AUTHOR

Author Photography by Gregory West

DR. STEPHANIE F. WEST is a Cornell University–trained veterinarian with management and teaching experience. She is currently a veterinary practice management consultant, supporting the optimization of efficiency in veterinary hospitals so that they can fulfill their missions to serve animals and the people who care for them. Her previous management experience includes serving as a senior hospital administrator with a national corporate veterinary group and as the CEO of a veterinary shareholder corporation, where she also was the executive director of their emergency clinic and their business-to-business wholesale buying group. She served as the director of hospital operations at a well-known Midwest college of veterinary medicine, was a tenured faculty member and program director of veterinary technology at a small northeastern university, and practiced veterinary medicine for many years at a well-respected feline practice.

Dr. Stephanie enjoys volunteering her time to support veterinary medicine on several professional boards and advisory committees. She was a top-ten national finalist for Practice Manager of the Year (2016) from *DVM360*/Veterinary Hospital Managers Association. The New York State Veterinary Medical Society has honored her with an award for Outstanding Service to Veterinary Medicine. In her spare time, she enjoys mentoring veterinary professionals and spending time with her husband and her cats, Purr-sephone and Satina Negra.